PRAISE FOR THE CONNECTION BOOK

"Fascinating, accessible and practically useful. *The Connection Book* will open your eyes to a layer of daily interactions you didn't know were there."

Jamie Simmonds, managing director, TheTin

"It is about using your personal talents and benefits when creating human relations. It sounds easy, but in reality it is one of the hardest things to master. Through 50 tips in *The Connection Book* you will receive the key to create these ever so important human relations that will accelerate your career."

Simone Andersen, journalist and author of *The Networking Book*

"Anyone and everyone will benefit from reading *The Connection Book* – practical, easy to read, yet so powerful in tackling today's number one challenge – communication. The simple layout and ease of reading almost disguise the depth of knowledge within. It's one to dip in and out of, leading to well thumbed pages as it's used over and over to fine-tune comms, both at home and at work. Anyone who wants to self-improve must read it!"

Jane Sunley, best-selling business author and founder of employee engagement experts, Purple Cubed

Published by
LID Publishing Ltd
The Record Hall, Studio 204,
16-16a Baldwins Gardens,
London EC1N 7RJ, UK

524 Broadway, 11th Floor, Suite 08-120
New York, NY 10012, US

info@lidpublishing.com
www.lidpublishing.com

A member of:
BPR
Business Publishers Roundtable
www.businesspublishersroundtable.com

Reprinted 2017

Printed in Latvia by Jelgavas Tipogrāfija

ISBN: 978-1-911498-41-4

Cover and page design: Caroline Li
Illustrations: Sara Taheri

THE CONNECTION BOOK

50 WAYS TO COMMUNICATE MORE EFFECTIVELY

EMMA SERLIN

LID

LONDON
MADRID
MEXICO CITY

NEW YORK
BARCELONA
MONTERREY
SHANGHAI

BOGOTA
BUENOS AIRES
SAN FRANCISCO

FOR OTHER TITLES IN THE SERIES...

CONCISE ADVICE LAB

SMALL BOOKS: BIG IDEAS

CLEVER CONTENT, DYNAMIC IDEAS, PRACTICAL SOLUTIONS AND ENGAGING VISUALS – A CATALYST TO INSPIRE NEW WAYS OF THINKING AND PROBLEM-SOLVING IN A COMPLEX WORLD

conciseadvicelab.com

CONTENTS

INTRODUCTION

Welcome to *The Connection Book*. This book is an exploration into communication and relationships. Within its pages you will find unique techniques and intuitive tools that will help you to build more authentic, powerful connections with people, in general and in specific situations.

How we relate to others effects almost everything we do. Take a typical day – from saying good morning to one's partner, the commute with strangers and the exchange with the person at the coffee shop, through to the meeting with one's team, bosses and clients and the evening out with friends, including the purchase of a bottle of wine en route. Connections and exchanges with people are central to all of these interactions.

Imagine a day when every one of those exchanges went really well. Imagine that in each one, you felt warm, articulate, friendly, that you made the other person happy or stimulated or impressed. It would feel like a pretty great day I suspect! And now, for just a minute, imagine the opposite. You alienate people rather than draw them in, sound self-absorbed rather than interested, come across as fuzzy rather than articulate, nervous instead of confident, and to top it off, have an argument with the guy in the wine shop followed by a blazing row with your partner. Pretty awful, right? Sadly, most of us have days like this. Sometimes, as the saying goes, we just got out of the wrong side of bed.

But what if I were to tell you it's all well within your control? That you can turn those exchanges into fulfilling connections, where you can make someone feel good, or do your idea justice, or turn an argument into an opportunity, as and when you want to? Well, it is possible. Using the tools in this book you can take control of the relationships and exchanges in your life, turning them into consistently positive experiences.

The Connection Book is based on the work we have done over the past nine years through my company London Speech Workshop, teaching effective communication and presentations skills to hundreds of clients, with backgrounds as diverse as the Middle East's equivalent of Oprah or MPs and teachers. This book will provide you with a range of skills, from a set of vocal and physical fundamentals, through to techniques for delivering more powerful presentations, building rapport, having more productive and satisfying meetings and turning potential conflict situations into peaceful, productive ones.

Please enjoy and practise any of these deceptively simple concepts that resonate with you. The more you open yourself to giving them a try, the more these ideas can change your life. And they will.

YOUR JOURNEY

This book is broken into six parts, each of those parts into five chapters, and each chapter offers an array of little gems, ideas, protein-packed paragraphs and helpful tips.

You could read it cover-to-cover or dip in and out, depending on which parts and chapters take your fancy. I would suggest, however, casting your eye over the more general chapters in the first part of this book, to give you some great tools to use from the get-go. That's why the book begins with fundamentals – a collection of ideas to get you into the head space of building powerful connections.

PART ONE

FUNDAMENTALS OF BETTER VOCAL CHARISMA

In this first section we explore some fundamental tools that will help you to build authentic connections. It's very difficult to connect if you sound insincere or robotic, for example. So this is about getting the vocal stuff straight. My colleagues and I start with the basics, literally vowels and consonants, as you can't build on a shaky foundation. From there we go on to sounding good through the use of emphasis, pauses and psychological hooks, which will help you feel grounded and confident when you speak, and come across as engaging and persuasive. After that, it's on to the art of delivery, which lies at the heart of connecting. These are some of the first tools to learn, and they'll have a massive impact straight away.

AN INTERESTING IDEA: THE VOCAL LANDSCAPE

One idea we love to share is that of the vocal landscape. The concept is that the way in which you speak – your volume, tone and how you use your voice – builds a vocal landscape in your listener's mind. So, the more interesting your voice is, the more compelling the landscape. It's a useful metaphor in terms of picturing the effect of your communication and being able to quickly assess how you are doing.

Most of us have been in lectures where the speaker drones on in a monotone, with no variation of pace or volume. It is so awful that, try as we might, we can't hold onto a single word or phrase, as if our brains are covered in ice and everything slides off. If no words or ideas have emphasis or colour, then the speaker is offering up no indication of which ideas or words really matter to them. This each chapter offers a barren, colourless landscape and, as a result, the speaker will struggle to hold their listeners' attention.

On the other hand, we have all heard speeches which make our pulse race and imagination flow, as if the words are mainlining straight into us. This is an example of a great vocal landscape, which provokes the listeners' feelings and gives them space to come up with their own opinions and responses. This speaker is directing their listeners' attention to the big ideas using intonation and emphasis, and, in doing so, creating a vocal landscape filled with colour, dimension and texture.

There are two brilliant things about creating an interesting vocal landscape: not only does it make what you are saying sound interesting, but it gives the speaker the power over what is created in their listeners' minds. The speaker uses their voice and way of speaking to indicate which words and ideas really matter, effectively fast-tracking the communication process.

THERE ARE THREE COMPONENTS TO CREATING AN INTERESTING VOCAL LANDSCAPE:

1. Words – the building blocks of words themselves, consisting of vowels and consonants.
2. How you say what you say – made up of emphasis, pausing, intonation and delivery.
3. What your body says – posture, gesture, facial expression and connection spaces.

CHAPTER 1: VOWELS - THE SOULS OF WORDS

Many people think of vowels as simply a set of sounds that make up a word. But they are so much more. Vowels can provide an opportunity to connect in communication. Why? Because they offer a space and time to interject your feelings. And feelings, when shared with others, build connections.

Vowels are pronounced with an open mouth and, as such, literally come from inside of a person. This means they can be coloured with all sorts of emotion to portray different meanings. Take, for example, the sound 'ahh'. Try saying it in five different ways; notice how easy it is to do and how each way can have a vastly different meaning.

So we can think of vowels as holding the soul of the word. By committing to it fully, you can harness the full potential of the word. This is one of the reasons why great actors and orators can have such an impact: they know the secret of showing their feelings through the vowels.

VOWELS AND EMOTIONAL RELEASE

If we keep our mouths closed when we speak, then the vowel sounds become clipped and less expressive. This will have one of two effects: either our feelings are forced to come out through our body language, or they are suppressed altogether.

The former issue is quite common with non-native speakers, who may not know how to channel their energy through vowels, so it comes out through strong (perhaps exaggerated) gestures. When the energy of these individuals is redirected into their vowels, their spoken communication is transformed.

The latter challenge, when emotion is suppressed, is more endemic in native English speakers, and can be connected to the clichéd English characteristic of the 'stiff upper lip'.

TRY IT FOR YOURSELF:

1. *Say 'I am so angry right now, I am in a rage' with all the energy you can muster, but with your teeth clenched firmly together.*
2. *Now try saying it again, with your mouth open and moving freely.*

Can you notice the difference in feeling?

The first is like you are stuck, unable to release your emotions, while the second is like an outpouring of emotion.

You might find that by opening your mouth more when you speak, you feel different – perhaps vulnerable or exposed, or as though you are allowing yourself to be seen in a way you haven't been seen before.

SHAKESPEARE, SOUNDS AND EMOTIONS

William Shakespeare was a composer of human emotions, creating great emotional symphonies that have tugged on the heartstrings of millions. His instruments were words, storylines, characters and sounds. If there are harsh consonants in the speech of a particular character, that will tell you something of their state of mind. If they have long vowels and soft consonants, it will imply that they are in a calmer, softer place. This means that if you read a Shakespeare play with an awareness of the sounds he used, you will find yourself on an emotional journey that The Bard carved out all those centuries ago.

For a great example of this, look for the actor Kenneth Branagh's 'Henry V – St Crispin's Speech by William Shakespeare' on YouTube. The speech is filled with long vowel sounds, which Branagh uses to pour emotion into his words. He incites his men to fight to the death, despite being outnumbered three to one. It's an address filled with emotion and, unsurprisingly, the vowels are stretched within an inch of their lives. Shakespeare knew that the best way to transmit emotion is through long vowels, and this speech is filled with them!

You can view Branagh's moving soliloquy here:
http://www.youtube.com/watch?v=s1Ulz-Qwnx8

CHAPTER 2: CONSONANTS - THE BUILDING BLOCKS OF LANGUAGE

Within our vocal landscape, consonants are the edges and outlines that hold things in place. They provide definition to our ideas; they stop the objects in the environment from merging into each other. While vowels hold the emotional content of what we are saying, consonants contain the emotion of the vowel. Consonants can be seen to represent accuracy, efficiency and, in a strange way, respect for the language.

Together, vowels and consonants make up a stereotypical English character: emotional yet restrained. For while we English are filled with emotion, we also like to be in control, especially of our emotions. Is that not so?

CONSONANTS AND THEIR ROLE IN BRITISH SOCIETY

In England, like it or not, speakers are judged by their accent, in terms of class, education and even intelligence. This is particularly focused around consonants, and muddled or missing consonants are the worst culprits. For example, if someone frequently drops *t's*, or switches *th* for *f* (as in 'fanks' instead of 'thanks') it can make a poor impression. While this may be unfair and frustrating, it is also a reality, so knowing how to pronounce consonants accurately can help shape the impression you wish to make.

CONSONANTS - AND PRECISION

Consonants can also convey respect for the word and the language itself. Take the words 'hate' or 'smart', 'sweet' or 'bitter'. If we want these words to have their full power, we need to express them with crisp consonants.

Words are powerful tools with sharp blades that can achieve precise goals. If we blunt that tool and throw it, do we still expect it to hit with as much finesse and precision? Of course not.

But before you feel concerned that every word has to be pronounced in its entirety, take comfort – there are actually only two situations where you really need to pronounce a consonant accurately:

Situation 1: At the end of an important thought.

Situation 2: In-between two vowels.

For example, if I said, 'An important thought,' and dropped the final T, it would sound sloppy. Similarly, if I said, 'It matters,' and dropped the two t's in the middle of the word 'matter', it would sound as though it didn't matter!

If you feel that you are prone to dropping or switching consonants, then read on for a little taste of how to improve your enunciation through some exercises and warm ups.

Try it for yourself:
Warm ups and tongue twisters are great for getting your tongue, lips and palate into gear. This is particularly useful if you tend to mumble or have a slightly muffled sound. If you are ever accused of being unclear, then performing these simple exercises for a few minutes a day over 21 days (the time it takes to build a new habit) will do you a world of good!

FACE

- Massage the jaw and face.
- Chew on an imaginary piece of toffee and imagine the toffee getting bigger.
- Make the face as small and then as big as you can. Do this three times.

TONGUE

- Clean the front and back of every tooth using the tongue three times.
- Point the tongue, holding it still for ten seconds. Then relax the tongue. Repeat three times.
- Circulate the tongue around the front of the mouth, ten times clockwise and ten times counter-clockwise.
- Push the tongue against your index finger, trying to push your finger away.

CONSONANT PRACTICE

- Sound out various consonants at high speed: b, d, g, b, d, g, (spoken very quickly, sounds like budiga); then do the same with p, t, k (putika).
- Now say the following two phrases ten times each with total clarity: lullaby lollipop; manilla vanilla.

LIPS

- Place some imaginary bubbles on the ceiling by making a soundless P with the lips - make the sound as crisp as possible. Now do the same thing but add sound to the 'P.'
- Make the following sounds, and repeat them ten times in sequence: www www www; vvv vvv vvv; bbb bbb bbb; wbw wbw wbw; bwb bwb bwb; wvw wvw wvw; vwv vwv vwv.
- With teeth closed, spread the lips into a smile, and then into a pouting shape. Do this fast, ten times.

TONGUE TWISTERS

Pick one of the following phrases and repeat it more and more quickly as you improve your accuracy. For an additional challenge, try and make it crystal clear while holding the knuckle of your thumb between your teeth.

- Whether the weather is warm or whether the weather is hot. We'll weather the weather whatever the weather, whether we like it or not.
- She sells sea shells on the sea shore. The shells she sells are shells for sure.
- I thought a thought. But the thought I thought wasn't the thought I thought I thought. If the thought I thought I thought had been the thought I thought, I wouldn't have thought so much.
- Sixty-six thistle sticks.
- Proper copper coffee pot.
- Upper roller, lower roller, upper roller, lower roller.
- Round and round the rugged rock the ragged rascal ran.
- Red lorry, yellow lorry, red lorry, yellow lorry.

CHAPTER 3: EMPHASIS, PAUSES AND HOOKS

Why is it that one person giving a presentation can sound like fingernails scraping down a blackboard, whereas another person is totally engaging, like spreading warm butter on toast? How do they do that? It is not magic. Quite simply, one person is making you work very hard whereas the other is doing all the work for you.

Much of 'this work' is made up of how they sound or, in other words, their intonation and melody. This is divided up into three important areas: emphasis – how to pick out important words that draw in the listener; pauses – how to use pauses or mini beats to divide up your thoughts, maintain control and interest; and hooks – a clever little tool called psychological hooks which help you add colour to your words.

EMPHASIS

We use emphasis to draw attention to the important words, so we can let our listeners know what is important. But which words do we choose? To put it simply, there is a word hierarchy – not all words are equal. There are words that hold information, and words that facilitate information but do not hold the information themselves.

The best communicators reflect this hierarchy with their voice, energy and breath. They emphasize only those words that contain meaning while letting other words - the grammatical words - take a back seat. This is because, in essence, English is an efficient language; its structure supports the speaker's use of energy only where it is needed. This is often where non-native speakers get stuck: they don't know about the built-in efficacy of the language, so they give each word equal weight. You can be perfectly fluent but, if you give each word equal weight, you're sacrificing the wonderful melody and full power of the English language. We can look at this more closely using a car metaphor.

FRONT-SEAT WORDS - These words hold information that adds to our understanding of an idea or a story. The difference between front-seat words like 'cat' or 'running' and back-seat words like 'is' and 'there' is that when you hear a front-seat word you can invariably picture it in some way, whereas a back-seat word holds little meaning out of context.

DRIVING-SEAT WORDS - These are chosen by the speaker to drive ideas home and are often words that the speaker has an emotional connection with. It's important to give more energy and power to these words, as they will get into the listener's head and convey what is important to the speaker.

BACK-SEAT WORDS - These are the in-between words, the bits and pieces that are almost invisible in a conversation. They are grammatical noises that populate our sentences to enrich their meaning - by spotlighting gender or tense, for instance. In and of themselves, they do not supply meaning. They include words like 'he', 'she', 'did', etc.

FINAL WORD IMPACT

English sentences are structured so that the impact of the meaning arrives with the final word. As such, the final word of the thought or unit is always important and needs to be emphasized. Look at the sentence below:

'An idea is nothing without its destination.'

If you remove the final word ('An idea is nothing without its.'), the sentence doesn't mean anything.

The sentence makes full sense only when you get to the final word, because it gives meaning to all that comes before it. So don't let a final word sink without a trace, as that will undermine the value of the entire thought.

TIP: Emphasis is more than just speaking louder. You can also linger a bit longer over a word, or go higher with your pitch to emphasize it.

PAUSES

Using pauses to divide up your thoughts is one of the most effective ways to share your ideas. We are not talking about long, empty pauses, but short beats that frame a unit of thought. This makes us sound steady and in control, which, in turn, helps the listener to process what we are saying and stay with us. In most cases, one unit of thought equates to one breath.

If we try to squeeze too many words into one unit or breath, then the listener will be unable to effectively absorb all of our ideas. This is what's often happening when it becomes difficult to follow someone. Their sentences are too long and they are packing too many words into one unit.

This uniting technique has so many advantages. It will stop you from getting tongue-tied or feeling as if you are running ahead of yourself and grasping for what to say next. It will give you time to connect with your listener, to think on your feet, to engage with vowels and inject some emotion into your words. You simply can't achieve that if you talk too rapidly.

Try it for yourself:
Read the following paragraph, which includes a short pause or mini-beat on each slash (/) and imagine that it is someone speaking to you. Notice how steady it now feels.

These units of thought / make the listener feel comfortable / and give you, the speaker, / time to process as you go / and, where necessary, / think on your feet! By using units / we can hold the hand of our listener / so to speak, / and ground ourselves in the present moment, / so we feel solid and in control. / This idea is at the very heart / of being an engaging speaker.

TIP: Unit breaks sit well after information words (front-seat words in the car metaphor) but not after grammatical words.

TIP: Unit breaks are not bound by punctuation, so even if we have a very long sentence, we can still break the thought into smaller chunks and help the listener to follow our meaning.

THE £10 BREATH
- RAISING THE VALUE OF YOUR WORDS

Remember that when we speak, we are making an implicit statement about the value we place on our words. A useful metaphor is that of the £10 breath.

Imagine that each unit of speech is worth £10 in value. Every time you break a sentence into smaller units, and deliver more incremental units, you increase the overall value of the sentence. If you speak a sentence without pausing, it is only worth £10. If you insert five pauses or units into the same sentence, it is worth £50. This corresponds with how much energy you are able to give it. If you are saying the whole sentence in one breath (and one unit), you are limited in what you can do – you simply don't have the breath to bring out certain words. If, on the other hand, you have inserted pauses, you have the breath to give a lot more energy to each unit, thereby raising the value.

So next time you find yourself talking at high speed without taking a breath, be aware of whether that is giving your thought sufficient value. Then slow down, add pauses, breathe and *raise the value of what you are saying*.

PSYCHOLOGICAL HOOKS

The next step is to use our voice to justify the pauses. Otherwise, it can sound as though we are stopping and starting for no apparent reason. We have to do something with our voice in each unit, to show that the unit makes sense on its own.

This can be achieved by applying some colour and tone to one word in particular in each unit. We call this a psychological hook, because it literally hooks the attention of your listener with your voice.

Psychological hooks can have a few wonderful results. In particular, they give the impression that you believe in what you are saying – that it is of value to you.

HOW IT WORKS: At any moment there is so much information around us that our brains have adapted to make snap decisions about what is really worth attending to. One great way of making this assessment is by using the information supplied by a speaker's tone of voice. If someone speaks in a dull monotone and seems bored by their own message, then the listener can justify switching off. But if someone believes a certain thing is truly amazing and reveals that to you in the way they speak, you will want to know about it! By putting colour into your voice as you speak certain words, you yank at the listener's attention and state that this is worth listening to.

TIP: Time to think. Psychological hooks can also buy you time to think if you are struggling to find your next word. You can do this by drawing out (lengthening) a vowel. In a high-pressure meeting, for example, this is a fantastic way to slow yourself down and buy time without getting flustered.

TIP: Keep it varied. To make your psychological hooks effective you need to do something different with your tone in each unit. If you use exactly the same intonation in each unit, such as raising your voice, it can begin to sound robotic.

TIP: Which words to 'hook'. Always put hooks on front-seat words, because they are the ones you want to draw attention to. If you draw attention to a back-seat (grammatical word), you are implying that it is important, which is usually not the case!

TIP: Multi-syllabled words. If you choose a multi-syllabled word over a simpler word, you must take account of the fact that it demands more processing time from the listener, and more breath to articulate. Otherwise it can easily become a word that gets lost as the listener tries to keep up. So highlight your multi-syllabled words with your voice in order to ensure that your speech makes its full impact.

CHAPTER 4: DELIVERY - REGULAR MAIL VS. SPECIAL DELIVERY

Giving an amazing speech to an audience of 100 people is pointless if you have your back turned to them. Delivery is about making sure your communication goes all the way to its intended destination. If your ideas don't hit their mark, you might as well be singing your heart out to an empty room.

It's a little like regular mail versus special delivery. Regular mail is the equivalent of a quick glance at your audience – 'it's probably arrived' – while special delivery offers the assurance that it absolutely gets to the destination. That's what we do with things we value, we make sure they get where they're going.

Good delivery boils down to three main concepts:

- Intention – you must intend for your message to reach your audience.
- Vocal gravity – using your voice to deliver your message.
- Eye contact – using your eyes to make sure your idea has been delivered.

INTENTION

Intention is defined as an act or instance of determining mentally to pursue some action or result. Whatever our intention, that is where our energy is focused. So when we're communicating, we need have our focus on the listener. If we focus our attention elsewhere – thinking about whether we will be okay, if people will like us – we've lost the power of intention. It's a simple idea but, bizarrely, one that so many speakers miss – particularly if they're reading from a piece of paper! Often their notes get the force of their attention as they forget to connect with their audience. So remember, it is crucial that your audience knows the story or speech is specifically for them and not a canned, generic spiel. If they feel irrelevant in the communication dynamic, then why should they carry on listening?

VOCAL GRAVITY

Your voice can go up in the middle of a thought, but it needs to come down at the end so that it lands decisively with your audience. Think of it as building a bridge between you and your listener. It starts with you, goes up a little in the middle, then comes down to arrive at your listener. Vocal gravity is essential. Otherwise it's like trying to deliver something to someone while reaching upwards. Not easy on you or your listener! This is why we don't encourage upward inflection (when your voice goes up at the end), as it's quite difficult to deliver an idea to someone if your voice is going up. You can read more about upward inflection and when to use it a little later in this section.

EYE CONTACT

When we make eye contact with another human, there is no doubt that we are making a connection with each other. The cliché of eyes meeting across a crowded room is such a powerful one because of this primal, interpersonal connection. Two people know, in that moment, that they are occupying a shared space in each other's minds.

Eyes also express intention. Think of aiming a bow and arrow at a mark on a tree. Imagine looking at the point on the tree that you hope to hit with your arrow, and pulling your arm back. Just before you let the arrow loose, can you feel what happens with your focus? There's an increase in attention and all other noises and sights fade out, increasing your chances of hitting your target. Using your eyes to deliver an idea, with the same intent you would use to shoot an arrow, adds power to your speech in the same way. If you don't look at the people you are speaking to, you have no idea if your words have hit their mark.

This does not mean you need to look at your audience or single listener continuously as you speak. You only need to look at them as you say the last few words of an important thought. As with the metaphor of the arrow and the tree, you don't take your shot and then look away!

This concept is so instinctive that, unless you know it consciously, you won't think of it even while you do it, and yet it single-handedly can make the biggest difference to whether an audience or listener feels engaged or not. So next time you are speaking to someone and want to hold their attention, make sure you look at them at the end of your thought, and feel the connection grow.

Try it for yourself:

Effectively delivering your spoken ideas or not is akin to talking at someone versus communicating with someone. This is when your intention, voice and eye contact combine to literally place your ideas in the hands of your listener or audience. When you connect in this way with the people you are speaking to, communication magic starts to happen.

Here's another simple exercise:

1. *Pick up a text.*
2. *Mark out the ends of the sentences that contain particularly important thoughts.*
3. *Mark a spot denoting a moment of direct, concentrated focus on your listener.*
4. *Now make eye contact at that spot every time you get to the last few words of an important thought.*
5. *If you want to make this more interesting, you can actually 'deliver' a physical object, so you get the sense of placing something with your listener. The cutlery drawer comes in handy for this! Pick up a knife, a fork and a spoon and literally deliver each, one by one, into the hands of your listener.*

CHAPTER 5: INFLECTION - WHAT GOES UP MUST COME DOWN

Have you ever listened to someone who raises the pitch of their voice at the end of every clause in their sentence? This can make listening tough going as you try to hold all the words in your mind until you finally lose the thread altogether. What they are doing is called upward inflection. It is typical of English teenagers and Australian speakers, and who can forget the California 'Valley Girl' dialect in all those movies from the '80s? If used too often, it can give the impression of immaturity and uncertainty, and make it difficult for the speaker to come across as authoritative.

There are only two occasions when we need to use upward inflection: for a list, and for a question that you don't know the answer to.

LISTS

The list inflection informs the listener that each item is simply one part of a bigger list and, therefore, not important in and of itself. It is the whole list that is of interest. Upward inflection is fine in this context, but when people say important things in the tone of a bulleted list, it's not so good! By using the same upward-swinging rhythm and tone with each item, the implicit statement is that they are all items that hold no particular value on their own. If the thoughts that make up a sentence or sentences are not important, as in a shopping list, then it's fine to recite them with a list-like tone. However, if those thoughts are important, then we need to reflect their unique, individual value with our voice.

SHOPPING LIST EXAMPLE: 'I'm going shopping (downward inflection). I'm going to buy potatoes (up), tomatoes (up), bath salts (up), chocolate (up) and a nice bottle of champagne (down).'

QUESTIONS

The other time we use upward inflection is if we are asking a question that we really want an answer to. It's fine to go up in pitch here because, in a sense, it is admitting that what you're saying isn't complete – it needs an answer to complete it. In this case it can be like reaching out to someone with a half-thought and needing a response to make it whole.

Example:
Are you okay? (up)
Yes, I'm fine. (down)
Should this go in the fridge? (up)
Yes, please. (down)

Sometimes you might use this inflection to show willingness or to connect, but it will not be useful to convey authority or to assert status. If we want to seem certain and sure of ourselves, then we need to deliver our thoughts using vocal gravity. This all may sound rather subtle, but you'd be surprised at how inflection can make a difference.

TIP: Get what you want. If you want someone to do something for you, ask a question with downward inflection (vocal gravity) and you will be more likely to get the response you want.

TIP: Build a bridge. If you are struggling to find vocal gravity, put your hand in an arc shape, facing away from you, as you speak the unit or thought, signifying a bridge between you and the other person.

TIP: Be the creator. Imagine you are God. Make statements like 'Then there was light' or 'Two plus two equals four' with complete and utter certainty. It's safe to say God wouldn't upward inflect!

TIP: Build rapport. If you want to relax someone, or if you feel you have been too high status and want to connect with them more, then upward inflection can be very useful.

PART ONE TAKEAWAYS

1. The concept of a vocal landscape is a useful metaphor to remind you how much power you have over the way your ideas are formed in another person's mind.

2. If you barely open your mouth when you speak, it's difficult to let any emotion out, and emotion is how we connect and inspire others.

3. You can drop some consonants and get away with it, but not in-between a word or at the end of a thought.

4. Avoid the two main pitfalls with consonants - dropping them and switching them.

5. Practise the vocal warm ups and exercises outlined in this section for five minutes a day and rid yourself of old habits.

6. Words that hold information and meaning need to have more emphasis than less-important grammatical words.

7. Using pauses or unit breaks is a brilliant tactic for dealing with nerves, and for buying time to convey your thoughts in a high-pressure situation.

8. Add a little bit of colour in your voice through information words – those 'front-seat' words that are central to the thought you want to convey – in every unit. This dash of colouration will serve as a psychological hook for your listener.

9. The best eye contact when 'delivering' to an audience is sustained for a beat at the end of a unit, which shows them you genuinely want to ensure that they receive, understand and appreciate the thought.

10. Focus on your listener or audience and make sure they receive your message through a generous blend of eye contact, vocal gravity and intention.

PART TWO

FUNDAMENTALS OF BETTER BODY LANGUAGE

You now have some helpful vocal tools. The idea of part two is to give you complementary physical devices for your tool box, so that you can do more, stretch further and ultimately achieve greater things with your communication.

In his book, *Silent Messages* (1972, Wadsworth Publishing), Dr. Albert Mehrabian, Professor Emeritus of Psychology at the University of California, Los Angeles, asserted that 93% of all daily communication is non-verbal. While this may not be entirely accurate, it makes an important point. We want to make sure that our body is saying what we want it to say. What we don't want is for our words to be saying one thing, our voice and manner conveying another, and our body to be demonstrating something entirely different! Fortunately, it is possible to become aware of the messages you are transmitting with your body language and then make sure they are consistent with your intended message. In Part Two of this book we also explore the importance of good posture, gestures and facial expression, and offer a powerful tool for giving you physical and vocal range.

CHAPTER 1: UNDERSTANDING BODY LANGUAGE

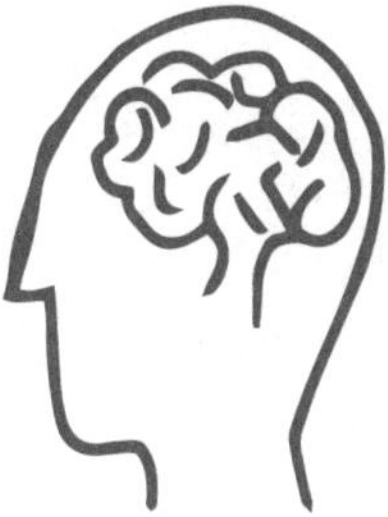

Understanding body language gives you more control over the impression you make. If, for example, you are feeling particularly nervous and defensive and about to go into a tough meeting, you can make sure your body language is expressing confidence and openness to help you make a positive impression.

Have a look at the box below. Think about where your habitual position is for each component. If you think any of your non-verbal communication is in the defensive column, try to make a conscious choice to change it. If you are not sure, take a moment when you're actively communicating to do a quick mental checklist. Where are your shoulders? What are your eyes doing? Perhaps you're usually in the confident column, but particular people or situations make you defensive. Try noticing when and where you move into the defensive zone, and what you habitually do when you are feeling defensive. Then, see if you can modify that behaviour.

Body	Defensive	Relaxed	Strong and confident
Posture	Shoulders rounded, bent over, small	Shoulders relaxed, not forward or back	Straight spine with shoulders back
Eye contact	Avoiding eye contact, blinking frequently	Light eye contact, sometimes flitting	Direct eye contact
Facial expression	Stiff, inexpressive face, jaw clenching, lip biting	Smiling, bright eyes	Warm and relaxed face
Gestures	Arms close to the body or no gestures at all, arms crossed in front of body	Flowing, easy gestures, relaxed and loose	Firm hand and arm gestures

TIP: Arm crossing tends to mean you are feeling defensive or self-protective. It is a real giveaway, and should be avoided unless you specifically want to signal that you are closed or wary.

TIP: Tilting your head to one side can signal trust or feeling safe with someone because by doing so you expose part of your neck, making you vulnerable. As such, it is unusual to tilt your head with people you don't feel comfortable with.

CHAPTER 2: POSTURE - SHOULDERS BACK, CHIN UP

If we straighten our spine and let our shoulders go back, we give the impression of openness, readiness and confidence. If our shoulders are slumped, it can give a dramatically different impression.

ONE INCH MAKES ALL THE DIFFERENCE

Look at the pictures below and ask yourself which individual you would want to fight in a boxing ring and which one you would like to hire as your lawyer. Chances are you chose the first picture for your opponent and the second picture for your lawyer. If this was a real-life situation, you might have no idea why those would be your preferences. You might think it was something they said, or that they appeared more confident, or perhaps they seemed weaker. The fact is, that little slump in the shoulders can make all the difference in terms of how we come across to others.

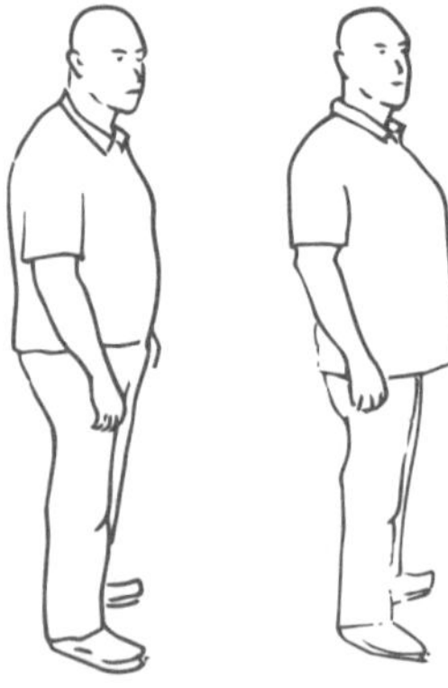

BAD POSTURE GOOD POSTURE

POSTURE AFFECTS SELF-ESTEEM

Studies have shown that good posture leads to increased self-esteem. Some research has shown that people experiencing depression felt markedly better after they made a concerted effort to improve their posture. A study by researchers at Ohio State University instructed subjects to sit up straight or to slouch; those who sat up straight had more confidence in their own thoughts, whether those thoughts were positive or negative.

HOW TO HAVE GOOD POSTURE

Step one: Centre of gravity

Experiment by pushing your hips forwards and then backwards, then find a centre point that feels comfortable between those two extremes. That's where you want them, as though a line is extending from your head through your body and down to the floor.

Step two: Alignment

Imagine a string is pulling upwards from the crown of your head to the sky and the rest of your body is hanging down from that string, dangling you into gravitational alignment. Your chin should feel balanced, as if it is resting nicely on a little table - not tilted upwards (which strains your voice as you have less direct access to your breath) or downwards (which will make you appear and possibly feel subdued or lacking in confidence.)

Step three: Shoulders

Now lift your shoulders to your ears and, rolling them back, let the shoulder blades slide down your back. Think about elongating the space between your ear lobes and your shoulders.

Next, gently stroke outwards with your hands horizontally across your chest to the edges of your shoulders and feel your chest opening to the world as if you had unfurling wings.

Now relax. You should feel comfortable, open and ready. Try walking in this position and see how it feels.

Try it for yourself:

Practise these steps daily, or whenever you are conscious of your posture. Do this for a week or two and see if you notice a difference.

CHAPTER 3: GESTURE - JAZZ HANDS

When we use our hands as well as our words and voice to tell our story, our messages become clearer, more engaging and more powerful. Using our body can bring an authenticity to our speech because the body is kinetically describing the scene as well. In addition, your listeners will remember the speech or story better because gestures can act as anchor points in memory. Using gesture also changes the tone and colour of your voice because physical movement sends signals to your brain – registering that you are physically engaged (and either relaxed or stimulated) – which in turn frees you up vocally. You might find that gesturing comes naturally to you, or it may feel a few steps out of your comfort zone and a bit awkward at first. Remember, it's not about changing your personality, it's about making a few significant changes to enhance your communication.

USING GESTURE

The first rule of gesture is to put yourself in a position where your body can get involved. If, for example, your hands are in your pockets or your arms are crossed, it's going to be difficult to get going. So begin in a state of readiness. Having your arms bent at the elbows allows your hands to easily spring to life, whereas if they are hanging down, there's more distance to cover. Give yourself permission to use your hands and arms.

TIP: Use your body to create the landscape for your communication. By changing position, you can signal a change of subject and you can separate ideas by moving to different areas of the stage.

POSITIVE HAND GESTURES

Firm fingers: It's important to keep your fingers quite firm and held together, so your energy reaches to the tips of your fingers.

Fists and strong hands: Both fists and solid hands give an impression of strength and determination, so make sure your hands have strength, particularly for meetings or presentations.

Open hands: A strong gesture also displays integrity.

Bent elbows: Have your arms bent at the elbows so you can move your hands easily and naturally.

HAND GESTURES TO AVOID

Floppy hands: Imagine you are watering roses in your garden; you don't want 'floppy hands' causing you to dribble water on your feet!

Clamped elbows: Avoid the elbows getting fused to your sides as this restricts your hands.

Arms straight and hanging down: This makes it difficult to raise your hands in order to gesture.

NERVES AND HOW THEY AFFECT GESTURE

When we are nervous, we can shut down and forget to use our bodies. This has a knock-on effect on the entirety of one's communication and can lead to less varied vocal tone, less facial expression, and a kind of clamp-down on the whole system. However, you can also remind yourself to use gestures when you are nervous, and this can have a liberating effect, freeing up your voice and your facial expressions as well.

Try it for yourself:

Hold one hand in the other, then spring both hands out, as if to say 'It's here!' This is an easy and relaxed position to start with. To practise, try reading a poem in front of a mirror, using your arms to shape the scene. Start to notice other people's gestures, and think about what you enjoy watching, what works and what doesn't.

CHAPTER 4: EXPRESSIONS - THE FACE TELLS IT ALL

So much of how we think and feel is expressed in our face. There are more muscle and nerve endings on the face than in almost any other part of our body, so it makes sense to learn how to use our facial expression to build better connections.

Many people use facial expression effortlessly; if you're one of them, then you may not need this chapter. However, there are many people who tend to express very little with their face. This may be cultural, or a long-established childhood habit. In some situations – playing poker for example – a deadpan expression can be very useful. Generally speaking, though, being able to use your facial expression as a communication tool is invaluable.

USE YOUR EYES TO BRING LIFE TO YOUR FACE

It is said that the eyes are the windows to the soul. So, if you don't use your eyes to communicate, it can severely restrict the communication process. This will have a knock-on effect on the range of your voice and the content of your speech.

Bright eyes tend to show active engagement, and a vibrant connection with what you are saying. They can also show sincerity. If you are prepared to look directly at someone and widen your eyes, you are in effect allowing them to peer into your thoughts.

Impassive eyes, on the other hand, can mean harder work for the listener. Dull or hooded eyes can give the impression that your mind is elsewhere – that you are tired, bored or worried.

BRIGHT, WIDE-OPEN EYES

Try opening your eyes really wide and notice how your eyebrows will automatically rise up with them. This can show a sense of excitement or wonder. If you use this bright-eyed face when greeting someone for the first time, it will have a far more positive effect than keeping your eyes hooded and smiling only with your mouth.

Still, be careful not to overdo it, as it can make you look overexcited!

ACTIVE EYES AND EMPHASIS

A simple trick to make your communication more engaging is to add emphasis to key elements in your speech by widening your eyes over the important words. This acts as a facial highlighter. The effect this has is twofold:

1. It draws your listener's attention directly to that word, making sure it has meaning and impact.
2. It pushes you to slow down slightly over that word which, in turn, makes it more effective.

This is particularly useful if you are a non-native speaker and find that people sometimes misunderstand you. Everyone recognizes 'eye language', and that will help signpost what's truly important for your listener.

> ***Try it for yourself:***
> *Begin to notice, in your personal interactions and when watching people on TV, how much eye movement there is. Notice where you are on the scale, what you like and what feels comfortable.*

CHAPTER 5: CONNECTING TO PEOPLE - FOUR CHOICES

Connection spaces give you choices in how you connect with people. There are four connection spaces, providing four different ways of connecting and coping with different people in different situations. The four connection spaces are: intimate, relaxed, performance and transformational. Each of these has its own individual kind of gesture and energy. They're simple, they're effective and anyone can use them. You will find that inhabiting each space changes the words you use, the expressions you make, and your volume, pace of speaking and tone.

Think of them as different outfits you might put on: the sharp suit for an important meeting, the soft cashmere sweater for a date, the well-worn tracksuit and cotton t-shirt for a lazy Sunday afternoon. Each of these will create its own virtual environment. Connection spaces act as shortcuts to those different outfits – and different aspects of ourselves, in seconds – without having to delve into the wardrobe!

Let's take a look at what constitutes the four connection spaces, and the situations where each of them might prove most useful.

THE INTIMATE CONNECTION SPACE

This is a gentle, sensitive space; a place to share something personal or to connect more deeply with someone. You are demanding higher-quality attention from your listeners. When you create this kind of space, you should be able to hear a pin drop. This space is good if you want to draw in your listeners, have them listen more intently and sharpen their focus.

POSTURE: Leaning in.
EYES: Sincere, focused, direct.
GESTURE: Small, simple, arms and hands close to body.
VOCAL TONE: Slow, low voice, limited tonal range.
CONTENT: Serious, secretive, delicate, private.
SITUATION: High stakes, serious, really connecting to people, sensitive.

THE RELAXED CONNECTION SPACE

This is a relaxed and more familiar place. It's an easy, confident space that you can use to chat with a friend, or even when talking to an audience of hundreds. Here you would use light, easy gestures, with a hand in the pocket or lightly gesticulating. The attention you have from your listeners is relaxed and open; they will feel engaged but not on high alert. This type of connection is useful for building an easy rapport, and when you wish to reveal your personality in a relaxed way.

POSTURE: Upright, relaxed.
EYES: Relaxed, moving around, in imagination and with the audience.
GESTURE: Relaxed gestures, hands in pockets, arms swinging by side, natural.

VOCAL TONE: Colourful, light, medium volume, warm.
CONTENT: Jokey, relaxed, friendly, anecdotal, informative.
SITUATION: Social situations, small presentations to colleagues, selected moments in a presentation to a larger audience and interviews.

THE PERFORMANCE CONNECTION SPACE

If you are speaking from this space you will make bigger movements, whether walking or stationary. Elbows will be at least an outstretched hand's-width from your sides, and hands will be moving in strong, expressive gestures. There is nothing timid or 'shrinking violet' about this space. Facial expressions are bigger, tone of voice has colour and range, and volume is louder than normal.

POSTURE: Upright, shoulders back. No slouching here!
EYES: Direct, wide, strong.
GESTURE: Arms away from sides, strong gesture, focused fingers.
VOCAL TONE: Strong volume, full use of vocal range, well-projected voice, emphasis. Speed is varied, alternating between slow and fast.
CONTENT: Higher stakes, important information.
SITUATION: Large presentations, pitches and product launches.

THE TRANSFORMATIONAL CONNECTION SPACE

This is the space inhabited by charismatic politicians, evangelical preachers and motivational speakers. The transformational space is about owning all the space around you and then some. It's about spreading your energy far and wide, with intention and direction. There is nothing intimate about this space; it is deliberate and powerful. Arm gestures will be extravagant, face will be free and, if you do get to this space, you're going to be pretty passionate so your body will be taking over anyway! The attention of the audience is totally with you – in fact, there is so much buzz around you that you don't know what energy is yours and what's theirs.

POSTURE: Upright.
EYES: Alive.
GESTURE: Huge.
VOCAL TONE: Loud, extensive tonal range.
CONTENT: Highest stakes, bigger themes, sense of purpose.
SITUATION: High-visibility public speeches, political rallies.

HOW TO USE CONNECTION SPACES

If you have an important event coming up, you can choose the space that will lead to the best possible outcome to meet your goals. For example, an actor meeting new agents, will want to be taken seriously, come across as confident and capable, and ultimately be signed up. Through practising the different spaces, the actor will find that the best one is likely performance with a bit of relaxed thrown in. From that place he will feel confident and empowered. Without the right connection space he may have gone in a little shyer and more subdued.

Remember, this is never about losing authenticity – it's about finding your range.

Try it for yourself:
Practise using the connection spaces to see what the different spaces offer you. If you find that you are naturally authoritative but struggle to make intimate connections, you'll benefit from practising the intimate space. Similarly, if you know you do well in one-to-one dialogue or small groups but find larger groups more challenging, then the performance space will be a useful resource for you. Simply pick up a text and try reading it in different connection spaces. If this works well, practise in a real, live conversation.

PART TWO TAKEAWAYS

1. Be aware of your body position – where your arms are, how far back your shoulders are – because people will read it!

2. Your posture matters. A one inch difference between shoulders slumped and shoulders back can be the deciding factor in whether someone connects with you or not. Stroke your shoulders back.

3. Your posture will make a difference to how you feel, so if you need a mood lift, help yourself along with good posture.

4. Gesture helps your audience to anchor ideas in their memory, as it tells a physical story.

5. Incorporating gesture will change your vocal quality and make you appear more connected to what you are saying.

6. Use your eyes to add life to your communication, and notice how people respond with more attention and easier engagement.

7. If you are tired, push yourself to more fully engage your eyes and face – it will make you feel more awake.

8. When you are in a different connection space, it changes not just your non-verbal communication but also the words you use and how you speak.

9. Use connection spaces to broaden your range and find new ways of dealing with difficult situations.

PART THREE

FUNDAMENTALS OF BETTER SOCIAL SKILLS

Why would you tell a particular person a story and not share it with someone else? Why do you find someone charming at a party and the next person a deadly bore? Why do you enjoy hanging out with one person more than another? It is because they make you feel good. They demonstrate that they are interested in you, through their body, voice and words. They have the gift of making you feel like you are the most important person in the room. That's why we like talking with them.

The real craft of making someone feel important is to pay them good-quality attention. And how do we do that? By noticing them, being likable and genuine, building rapport and, probably most important of all, being a good listener. You may think this is something we all know how to do innately, but for many people the art of listening is not a regular habit. Many are better at half-listening while doing something else, or listening while thinking about themselves ... or in fact not really listening at all.

CHAPTER 1: I MAKE, YOU MAKE, WE MAKE CONNECTIONS

Making someone feel important is one of the most effective ways of building a connection with that person. It makes the recipient feel good and, in turn, fosters mutual respect. However, it's important to be genuine. You can't make someone feel important while thinking they are insignificant. The best way to get to this head space is to tune in to the uniqueness and complexity of each individual. And the more we appreciate their uniqueness, the more we can step into an exchange with a genuine sense of curiosity and interest.

NOTICE OTHER PEOPLE

People love to feel noticed. Numerous studies have shown that people are motivated and work harder when they feel attention and an interest from others. You can 'notice' people in so many ways, from saying yes to invitations and remembering important occasions, to referencing something they said or complimenting an outfit or hairstyle. If you can show someone that you are interested in them, you'll go a long way towards making them interested in you.

DON'T ACT SUPERIOR

To some degree or another we are all driven by our egos, yet if our aim in a conversation is to feed our egos, then it's difficult to build a genuine connection. If we have a healthy dose of self-assurance, we can go into a conversation curious and open. But if our egos are underfed, and we are driven solely by self-interest, then interactions can easily become an exercise in ego-gratification. Watch for this in your exchanges; if there is a whiff of one-upmanship, you might be in the throes of ego gluttony. Just take a step back and remember this: one of our most effective ways of impressing someone is to let them know we are impressed by them.

GO IN WITH A POSITIVE ATTITUDE

The attitude with which you enter a conversation is also quite important. If you expect a person to be warm, honest and open, then chances are they will perform accordingly. If, on the other hand, you expect your listeners to be boring or snobbish, then you are more likely to get the expected response. So check in with yourself and get a handle on your attitude; if you notice a negative thought, try to swap it for a positive one. At the very least, assume the right posture and facial expression, for as we know, you can change how you feel and relate to others by changing your body language.

FINDING THE RIGHT ENERGY FOR YOUR LISTENER

If you are walking with a 90-year-old woman with a hip replacement, you would slow down ... right? Communicating is much the same. If someone is speaking slowly and with low energy, then you will be hard pushed to build rapport if you're rattling on at high speed. You want to make an effort to meet them where they are in order to connect.

You will find that by simply switching on your awareness of how the other person is speaking, you can assess what tone of voice, pace and volume suits the situation. As long as you are in the general ball park, you will be en route to building rapport.

USING QUESTIONS TO BUILD CONNECTIONS

Questions are powerful rapport builders because a genuine question is like a statement of interest, and that marks the beginning of a connection. A question conveys to the other party, 'I want to know what you think' or 'I want to know more about you.'

There are three types of questions:

OPEN QUESTIONS: These require more than one-word answers. They leave the other individual space to talk. They begin or include words like 'how', 'what' or 'why'. For example, 'How do you feel about football?' Open questions can be more powerful than closed questions because you are inviting the other party to open up, share and connect.

FOCUSED OR YES/NO QUESTIONS: These get down to the nitty-gritty of it. They usually require a single-word answer or a simple phrase. They begin with words like 'do you', 'are you', 'will you'. If you get the tone right, they can open things up. For example, 'Do you like football?' But beware of closed questions if you want to build rapport, because they don't encourage a long or meaningful response!

PARAPHRASING QUESTIONS: These help to make sure you understood correctly. They are about repeating the idea back to the speaker. The speaker can be very powerful in terms of showing that you have been listening and have understood. They also encourage the other person to open up more on the topic. Therapists use this type of question a lot. For example, 'So you said you dream of being a footballer...?'

CHAPTER 2: THE POWER OF SMILING

A genuine smile can, as the old cliché goes, light up a room. It certainly can light up a face, and make a plain-looking person beautiful in the space of a second. If you can use your smile to make a first impression on someone, you will be surprised by its power. But the smile has to be genuine to be really effective.

THE SCIENCE OF A SMILE

When you smile a genuine smile, your eyes will appear half-shut. This is because the muscles around the eyes, called the orbicular muscles, contract. Therefore if you see someone smiling and it doesn't reach their eyes, you know its not a genuine smile.

A genuine smile has been so widely researched by psychologists, it actually has its own name, after the person who discovered it. Its called a Duchenne smile. Scientific studies have shown a genuine smile elicits more positive responses from the receiver, and often provokes a genuine smile in turn, even between strangers. Not only does a genuine smile have a positive effect on people receiving it, but as it is linked to the part of the brain that manages positive emotions, we also know that it can make the smiler feel good too!

Nice huh?

Genuine smiles are good for making an instant positive impression. We like genuine smilers more and we want to spend more time with them. So when you find yourself drawn to a smiley person, remember people are drawn to you for the same reason. A good case for becoming a genuine smiler!

Some people won't feel comfortable smiling at strangers, or may feel it undermines their authority. In the end, each person must decide what is right for them. As with everything in this book, there is no 'right way' but there are tools and choices. If you have the tools, you can make the choice.

SMILING AND ITS PROVEN LINK TO WELLBEING

A study by psychologists Dacher Keltner and LeeAnne Harker from the University of California, Berkeley, analysed the smiles of 114 women in their 1960 university yearbook photos. All but three of the young women smiled. However, 50 had Duchenne smiles and 61 had non-Duchenne smiles.

Thirty years later, those in the genuine smile group were more likely to have gotten and stayed married, and had higher evaluation scores for physical and emotional wellbeing. You can read more about Keltner and Harker's research here:
http://psychcentral.com/blog/archives/2010/11/30/smile-big-youre-going-to-have-a-good-long-life/

Try it for yourself:

Have a look at the pictures below and see if you can recognize the Duchenne smile. If it helps, ask yourself who you would prefer to sit next to at a dinner party. It will likely be the genuine smiler.

CHAPTER 3: LISTENING - WITH YOUR BODY

When someone actively listens, they are giving lots of non-verbal signals that they are interested in what the speaker is saying. Eye contact, smiles, open body language, small filler sounds – all of these make up active listening. If none of these are present, then it can get pretty uncomfortable for the speaker. However, if active listening does happen, the speaker will usually respond like an unfurling flower; they will give more information, become more colourful and expansive, and more receptive to the listener. The following five steps are important to actively listen.

STEP ONE: EYE CONTACT.

This is about having your eyes on the speaker, being attentive to them and ensuring they are the sole focus of your attention. If the listener looks away, the speaker can lose confidence, as they assume the listener is not interested.

TIP: Tempting as it may be, try not to multi-task when listening.

STEP TWO: ACTIVE EYES

Allow your eyes to respond to what the speaker is saying. Let your eyebrows move, keep your eyes alert, and open them wider if you hear something particularly interesting or surprising. Don't allow your eyes to become vacant, stare into the middle distance or switch off entirely. The person speaking can tell instantly, and it is a sure-fire way to break rapport. It is the listener's responsibility to keep eye contact with the speaker.

TIP: It's the speaker's responsibility to break eye contact every so often so it doesn't become a staring match. But if they don't, you can!

STEP THREE: NODS AND OPEN BODY LANGUAGE

Nodding is a great way to build rapport and state without interruption that you are listening and interested. Couple the nod with a slight smile or widen the eyes for even more powerful rapport-building. Face the individual where possible with your body, which will make them feel they have your full attention. (It is fine for your legs to be pointed in a different direction, as long as your torso is facing them.)

TIP: Avoid crossing your arms or slumping and rounding your shoulders.

STEP FOUR: TONE

Using tone and colour in your voice is a great way of showing interest. Let your tone be warm and resonant, and connected to your breath and diaphragm. Feel the difference if you use a clipped voice that comes from the back of your throat. This will often happen when a person is nervous – the throat constricts and the voice becomes cold and abrupt as there is no access to the diaphragm.

TIP: To free up your voice, try putting a hand on your belly, breathing into your hand, and making some noises from there like hums or counting. You should feel the muscles under your hand contract.

STEP FIVE: SOUNDS AND WORDS

Using little affirmative sounds and words shows the speaker you really are engaged. If this isn't your norm, it might feel a bit odd at first, but you will find it natural with time and practice. Good sounds and words to use are 'uh-huh', 'yeah', 'really', 'ahh', 'great', 'good', 'mmm' etc. It's also useful to paraphrase back what you are hearing at selected points, or to make a small affirmative comment.

TIP: Use affirmative noises on the phone when you don't have eye contact; your sounds show you are engaged and interested.

Try it for yourself:
Try listening to someone using the elements from each chart, and see their reactions. You could try it with a friend. You will find that behaviours on the non-active listening chart shut people down. So if you don't want to build connections, its the one to use.

ACTIVE LISTENING CHART

Body language: open	Verbal language: soft, fillers	Tone of voice
Open gestures Smiles Warm eyes Nods Mirroring the speaker's movements Relaxed	Okay Sure I understand I see where you're coming from Great Ahh Mmmm	Warm Low Soft and slow From the diaphragm Bright and chirpy

NON-ACTIVE LISTENING CHART

Body language: closed	Verbal language: negative, direct	Tone of voice
Closed gestures No smile Unmoving eyes Crossed arms Body turned away Avoidance of eye contact	No You've got it wrong I disagree You statements: You said; you did Factual statements: That isn't the case That's rubbish Silence	Sharp Monotone Quick and clipped From the throat

CHAPTER 4: LISTENING - WITH YOUR HEAD

Active listening is a powerful way to show someone you are engaged. But there is more to listening than just building rapport. There is also the small matter of what you actually 'hear'. Each of the three levels of listening provides a different type of information while enabling the listener and speaker to build varying degrees of connection. This helps both parties really hear what is going on.

LEVEL ONE LISTENING

The first level is listening to someone with ourselves in the forefront of our minds. So when the speaker says something, we think about how it relates to us. Level one listening is from the ego. Whether to berate or promote oneself, it is always self-oriented.

This does not mean it is a bad level of listening, and it can work well for building rapport as you share similar stories and experiences. At the same time it's important to avoid spending all of one's time here, as eventually a speaker could feel ignored.

LEVEL TWO LISTENING

This is when you listen to the speaker and see links between their words and things they have said or done previously. It can be as simple as enjoying what they share, laughing along with them and commenting on what they are saying. You develop an analytical understanding of the person and become increasingly curious about them. This is great because level two listening is really about the individual you are speaking with.

LEVEL THREE LISTENING

When you listen at level three, you drop down into your body and become like a listening instrument. In particular, you will notice the speaker's breath, tone of voice, the speed at which they speak and their enthusiasm levels. You can take notice of their posture and their body language, their facial expression and level of eye contact. Your body and feelings can give you lots of information about how the speaker is feeling. If, for example, you notice your own breath is quick and you feel uncomfortable, chances are they feel uncomfortable too. By tuning into your level three reading of a situation, you can bring in an intuitive layer to your relationships which will serve you incredibly well.

Try it for yourself:
Next time you are in a social group or if someone is telling a story, notice which level you are in and take a moment to tune into your level two and level three reading of the situation. Look at the chart below to see some examples of the thoughts of a listener in each of the levels.

LEVELS OF LISTENING CHART

Speaker says:	Level one listening	Level two listening	Level three listening
'I'm terrible at team sports. I'm always last to be picked. It's awful.'	How awful. Thank God I'm never last to be picked. I couldn't handle that.	She says she's terrible, but she repeatedly puts herself in team sport situations. I wonder why.	Her breathing is fast, she said 'awful' with lots of energy; she seems distressed. I wonder what 'awful' means to her.

CHAPTER 5: 'I JUST CALLED TO SAY …'

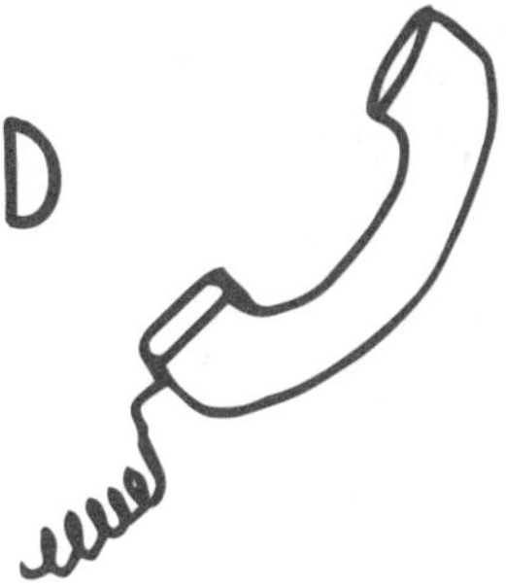

On the phone, your voice is all you have to make an impression so, if the call really matters, try and create a situation that will allow you to be at your best.

POSITION

The listener might not be able to see your body, but your physical position matters. If you are tangled up in a folded position or, if your shoulders are hunched or your arms crossed. Your voice will probably sound more strained (bad posture means you can't reach your diaphragm) and a folded body adds tension to your voice, thinning it out. So, sit comfortably with your body relaxed and a straight spine so you can take deep breaths.

ATTENTION

It is so easy to get caught up in doing more than one thing at once but, if the call is important, try not to multi-task. People can hear it in your voice when you are only half present, and most people will start to shut down as a result. Not only that, but you can miss subtle shifts in their voice, or even whole sentences.

One drop of inattention and you can lose the person on the other end of the line. Yes, you can coax them back out, but who knows the damage done.

ATTITUDE AND ENVIRONMENT

Make sure that you are in the right head space for this call. Since you can only use your voice and your mind, you will need to concentrate to make sure you get the desired outcome. One nice trick is to consciously step into a different zone – for instance, the strong and confident zone – as if you were engaging in an important meeting with that person.

SMILE ON THE PHONE

People can hear a smile in your voice. When someone calls, if you sound happy to hear from them, it creates the fertile soil of receptivity. If, on the other hand, you sound disappointed, then the whole conversation is back-footed. People sense these things subconsciously, so they may feel happy or disappointed and not be sure why. The initial feelings someone connects with at the start of a call can have an enormous effect on the outcome of a conversation.

TONE AND TENOR

Be aware of your tone on the phone. For women, a higher tone is more informal and girly, while a lower tone is more professional and authoritative. Although men tend to have less vocal range than women, it is the same for them. Higher tones in men can be lighter, and make them seem more approachable, but come across as less commanding. Lower tones are perceived as more masculine and associated with authority. See if you can adjust the pitch of your voice to suit your needs in the conversation.

PART THREE TAKEAWAYS

1. To build a connection, it helps to match or move towards the energy of the person you are speaking with.

2. Get curious about the speaker – see them as genuinely important and take an interest in discovering what makes them unique.

3. Use your smile to make a positive first impression and build rapport.

4. Smiling is not necessarily suited to all situations, but you can always make your eyes warm and alive when smiling is not appropriate.

5. Smiling has strong biological triggers in both the smiler and the receiver, and is, therefore, a powerful tool.

6. If you are tired, push yourself to engage through your facial expression; it will make you feel more awake.

7. Use head nods, open body language and filler sounds to actively listen.

8. Learn to listen on level three so you can read the nuances in someone's body.

9. Don't multi-task when speaking on the phone; focus intently on the other party.

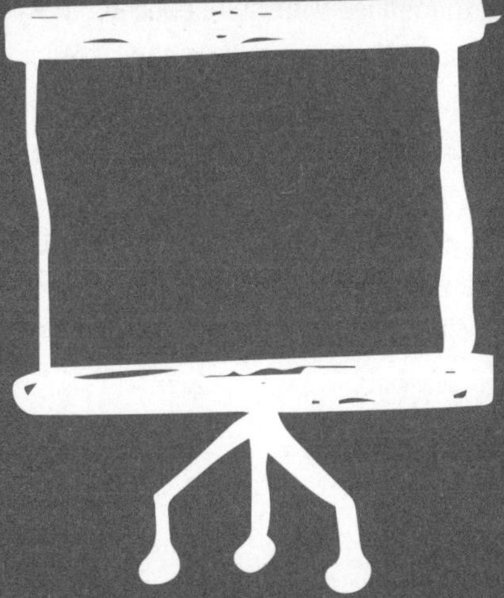

FUNDAMENTALS OF BETTER PRESENTATIONS

Far too many people find the prospect of giving a presentation daunting. An equal number dread sitting through presentations because of past experiences with dull speeches that left them none the wiser. Yet presentations are a huge part of many people's lives, so we need powerful tools to make presentations with confidence and achieve the desired results.

A presentation's writing should be powerful, engaging and get the point across. The physical delivery should feel fresh, alive and full of energy. The following five chapters will help you achieve this and more.

CHAPTER 1: PRESENTATIONS - CREATING SOMETHING SPECIAL

START WITH YOUR OBJECTIVE

To avoid waffling and going off topic, clearly define the objective of your presentation beforehand. Think about what effect you want to have on your audience. Do you want them to come away feeling inspired? Delighted? Motivated? Do you want them to buy the product, vote for you or change their life in some way? Every slide or spoken point should clearly refer back to the objective.

TIP: While there will be an overall objective, for a longer presentation there may also be smaller mini-objectives which can also have their own structure, as outlined below.

A GOOD STRUCTURE

There is a straightforward structure that works for most presentations and you can vary it to suit any occasion, situation and setting. It should be shaped into a sequence of: problem, solution, evidence, summary.

Problem

This might be a problem for your audience or a problem you are trying to get your audience to engage with. Whatever it is, there is usually a problem. (That's life!) It can be described in story form, or as a case study with a powerful hook.

Solution

This could be a quick fix, or a longer, more academic information piece. Ensure that you show how the solution works and how it will address the problem. This is the time to be an expert.

Evidence

Whether it's a pitch or an information-based presentation, you will need to offer the evidence to back up your point and establish trust and credibility. Evidence is needed so an individual can make decisions with both their head and their heart. Use qualitative evidence (i.e. stories) to appeal to the heart and quantitative evidence (i.e. statistics) to appeal to the head.

Summary

Finish with a brief summation of their problem and why you believe you can help. To round off your presentation you can also mention your values or what is driving you.

TIP: Use numbers or map the presentation so it's clear to follow. For example, "there are three strong arguments supporting this theory. I shall run through each of these in turn."

ENRICHING THE STORY

In order to connect with people, we need to show them a bit of ourselves, to make things personal, and ideally infuse our storyline with a palpable sense of emotion and humanity. This shouldn't be overdone, but sideline it at your peril.

CHAPTER 2: PRESENTATIONS - DELIVERING WITH PIZZAZZ

When it comes to delivering your presentation, it is important that you remember the essentials of making the right impression with both your body and your voice.

TAKING YOUR SPACE

As we know, first impressions count, so those first moments are crucial. Hold your shoulders back, your head upright and your chin level as you take the stage or stand up to speak. Next, take a moment to adsorb your space before you begin. This will ground you and let the audience see you and you see them. It's a subtle thing, but it will help calm your nerves and is a great way to connect with the audience. A smile or a nod are also excellent ways to make that all-important connection. Always remember that they want to enjoy their time listening to you, so they actually have a vested interest in you doing well!

EYES IN PRESENTATIONS

You may not know your presentation by heart and, as such, will likely need to read from the notes you have prepared. When reading, of course, you can't make constant eye contact and you don't want to either. It pays to remember that eye contact is about quality, not quantity.

The place for 'quality' eye contact is the final few words of the sentence or important point. At these points, hold the gaze for a moment, as if you are checking with the audience to confirm that they have received your message. This makes a psychological statement to your audience, conveying that you want them to receive and understand each point. And they will start to feel as though you really care.

Unfortunately, people often get this wrong. They look up in the middle of their text, and then look down at the end of their sentence to grab the next sentence. This makes entirely the wrong statement – that they are checking to see if people are still listening. Not the best impression to make!

TIP: Presentation preparation – When preparing for your presentation, underline the key points and draw a little eye symbol next to the final words of these points. This is where you should make eye contact to have the most impact. Remember, you're going for sustained eye contact, with intention.

TIP: Eye contact with a large audience – When you have a large audience, sharing your eye contact with different parts of the room is a good idea. A reliable rule of thumb is to spread the wealth from left-front to left-back, middle-front, right-back and right-front. Or, simply scan left, right, middle.

CONNECTION SPACES FOR PRESENTATIONS

Use connection spaces to build, shape and give dimension to your presentation. This will help your audience to remember content and stay engaged. To do this, mark up different sections in your presentation with your own relevant connection spaces.

If this feels a bit tricky, ask yourself what your goal is for each section. What do you want the audience to feel? Then match to the connection space that feels most appropriate. For example, you might use intimate to build intrigue, performance to excite and relaxed to make people feel at ease.

HOW TO ANSWER QUESTIONS

Always take a moment to acknowledge and compliment the question – it makes people feel recognized and, if it is a particularly challenging question, showing them you are genuinely open to engaging with it will instantly soften them. Not only that, but it changes the dynamic, and allows you to feel more in control rather than at the mercy of the questioner. Moreover, it will help ensure that the entire audience is involved, which will keep everyone focused and engaged.

If you don't know the answer, don't try to hide or pretend that you do instead, it may be appropriate to offer a straight-up, 'I don't know.' You can then immediately reframe the question, which is a great way of showing your willingness to learn. As long as you are open about not knowing, this technique leaves virtually no room for another person to counter-attack. If the question is complex, ask for a moment to jot down your thoughts. (See the tools in the

Fundamentals of Better Meetings section of this book for more on this.) What you must not do is react from a place of panic.

TIP: Always give yourself a moment to think when asked a question.

USING TECHNOLOGY FOR PRESENTATIONS

Make sure you know what facilities and equipment will be available at your meeting location. You will probably be using your laptop, so test everything in advance and have the cables needed to link to a projector. But don't rely on the technology to deliver a brilliant presentation – have clear notes, bring along a backup print-out of your slides, and be prepared to talk it through. If technology lets you down, start with a strong statement to give your audience a good first impression.

CHAPTER 3: PRACTICE DOES MAKE PERFECT

This seems obvious, but is often overlooked: there is nothing like practice to get you ready for an important presentation or speech. Practising in front of a mirror or with a colleague will help you to become familiar with it, build muscle memory and identify any rough spots. If you want practice for speaking in general, join a speaking club or use the techniques below and you will quickly improve.

1. Remind yourself of your overall objective and what, for you, is the best possible outcome of this speech. As you read through the material, make sure you feel attuned to this.

2. Read through your prepared remarks and look for key words or phrases that are particularly important. Highlight or underline these; later you will be highlighting them with your voice and gestures.

3. Mark out little pause points after big ideas – this is where you will be connecting with your audience through eye contact.

4. You can now do the first practice run. Be aware of the key points you want to deliver. Committing a handful of those important moments to muscle memory will be helpful when you actually deliver the speech.

5. While practising, you may have become aware of different energy opportunities, where you move from one connection space to another. By marking these different spaces in your speech, you will ensure that a range of gestures are used and keep things interesting.

6. If you want to deliver from memory, use an outline of single-word bullet points that act as reminders. You should avoid superfluous points. Having one or two of those points will be okay, but with any more there's a chance that your audience will get lost.

7. If your presentation is divided into several sections, make sure you know the most important point or two you want to make within each part, and any key words or phrases linked to each point. Make sure these are underlined and use your gestures, tone and emphasis to highlight these ideas and get them into your listeners' heads.

8. Now you can practise the entire speech, either in front of the mirror or to a willing observer. If you are able to have an audience, take notice of when they seem engaged and when they are not. At the end, ask them about their levels of engagement at different points and what they got out of it, and see if that aligns with your objectives.

CHAPTER 4: OVERCOMING NERVES - EVEN GANDHI GOT NERVOUS

Some people are completely at ease when they speak to an audience, while nerves get the better of others. But fear of public speaking, known as glossophobia, has been found in hundreds of studies to be people's number one fear, ranking even before fear of death.

Whether we have a full-blown fear or some nervous discomfort when speaking in public, it helps to have some ideas and tools at hand. A first useful step is to remember that there is rarely a rational basis for our fears. The strong fear we have is more likely to be a left over primitive instinct from hunter-gatherer days, when being singled out and stared at by a large group of fellow humans could easily pose a survival risk. Obviously now, standing up and speaking to a crowd, whether to ten or ten thousand, is unlikely to pose any actual risk to your survival.

While this realization won't eliminate the jitters, it will help you to get a grip and not take them too seriously. The good news is the more we engage in public speaking, the easier it gets. Read through the techniques and tools below and try out the ones that resonate with you.

1. CONNECT WITH YOUR NEED TO SPEAK

Some of history's greatest speakers were in fact terrified of public speaking, including Abraham Lincoln and Mahatma Gandhi. Both overcame this dread because their need to speak was greater than their fears. If you really want to communicate your message, embrace your need to speak.

Look at your prepared remarks and ask yourself:

- What are your goals for the audience; what are you giving to them? Will they be moved? See something in a new light? Have relief from pain or fear?

- Come back to the places in your speech that really deliver on these goals and tune into them. They are gems you will be placing into the hands of the audience.

2. FOCUS ON PRACTICAL DETAILS OF COMMUNICATION

Modern psychology tells us that we can't think two opposing thoughts at the same time. Try thinking of something sad while holding a grin. It's not easy. That's because your brain is receiving signals that it's happy. If panic sets in during a presentation, simply focus on emphasis, or delivery, and let that shift your mind away from fear-based thoughts. If negative thoughts creep in, bat them away like a fly and focus on your listeners.

3. VISUALIZATION

Some people are sceptical about visualization but scientific research has confirmed that it is, in fact, a valid cognitive tool. Psychologists have found that by imagining a physical process, you can build neural pathways in your brain that are almost exactly the same as if you had actually completed the activity!

Try visualizing yourself calmly getting out of your seat and walking onto the stage, looking at the audience and delivering your speech. Take it all the way to the applause and your sense of triumph. At points, you may start to feel anxious - this is fine, and shows you are in the imagination zone - but you have control! Simply rewind a little and do it again until you don't feel the nerves.

This is an incredibly powerful technique and is well worth the concentration it requires. There is a lovely anecdote about a concert pianist who was jailed for nearly a decade, and when he got out he was even better at playing his instrument than before. People asked him how he did it, and he told them it was by practising every day - in his imagination.

4. GOLDEN BALL

Imagine a ball of gold melting in your belly. Let its warmth spread down your legs and radiate up through your chest. With each breath you take in, the ball melts further. With each out-breath, the gold oozes through your body. Roll your shoulders slowly; let the gold ease into your neck. Open your chest and roll your shoulders back. Stretch your arms out. You can do this sitting in a chair just before you need to get up to do the presentation.

5. POWER GESTURE

It has been proven that if you stand in a power position for two minutes, you will significantly reduce the cortisol stress hormone in your system and elevate your energizing testosterone levels. So before a presentation, go somewhere private and stand with your arms outstretched and legs open and firmly planted on the ground. Two minutes later, you will feel different. (To understand this better, watch social psychologist and Harvard Business School professor Amy Cuddy's compelling Ted Talk on the science of power gestures).

6. MEET YOUR CHIMP

In his book, *The Chimp Paradox* (2015, Random House Export), English psychiatrist Steve Peters asserts that we are made up of two parts: the chimp and the adult. The chimp comes from the primitive limbic brain and is defined by base appetites and the fight-or-flight response. The adult, on the other hand, comes from the rational, higher functioning cerebral cortex. In high-pressure situations the chimp can get in the way, taunting us with our worst fears. He is the proverbial 'monkey on your back'.

So, according to Peters, we need to recognize who is doing the talking. If it's the chimp, simply ask yourself what your adult would say. The adult is usually more grounded and level-headed, and helps put our fears into perspective.

7. MINDFULNESS

You are feeling nervous, your heart is pumping and your breathing is fast, but by acknowledging this distress, half of its sting seems to dissipate. With this technique, you take notice of and label each of your physical symptoms in your mind. You are mindful of them, without judging them or fighting them. Awareness, in and of itself, can be a potent antidote to what troubles you.

8. IMAGINE YOUR AUDIENCE IS FASCINATED

Simply imagine that the audience is fascinated by what you are saying. If you hear any counter-thought, kick it out and replace it with the image of their thrilled faces. They are hanging on your every word. Start having fun with your speech and taking the time you need. Chances are the audience will pick up on this positive energy and become increasingly interested. Positivity tends to feed on itself, fuelling a virtuous circle.

CHAPTER 5: DON'T SCREW UP! TOP TEN THINGS TO AVOID

Avoid these negatives and you'll be doing really well!

1. **A WEAK OPENING**: Shuffling papers, fiddling with your laptop, dealing with technical problems, an incoherent opening line.

2. **STATEMENTS THAT DIMINISH YOUR CREDIBILITY**: I hope this isn't boring; I put this together at the last minute; I'm not really an expert on this but ...

3. **COMPLICATED JARGON**: You are aiming to communicate, not confuse.

4. **WAFFLING**: It's not about counting the words but making the words count.

5. **LACK OF STRUCTURE**: If your presentation wanders, so will your audience's attention.

6. **POOR BODY LANGUAGE**: Slumping, pacing, shuffling, hands in pockets, back to the audience, curved shoulders, crossed arms.

7. **LACK OF EYE CONTACT**: Looking at the PowerPoint, your papers or your shoes instead of being intently focused on the audience.

8. **OVERWHELMING THE AUDIENCE**: Don't give too much information, use arcane terminology or overwhelm them with irrelevant detail.

9. **OVER-RELIANCE ON THE SLIDES**: Use your slides to add value, but don't expect them to be the value!

10. **NOT HAVING EVERYTHING YOU NEED**: Before giving your presentation, write a list of everything you might need – audio-visual equipment, a pen, an illustrative prop, handouts, etc. Being unprepared is never a good look!

PART FOUR TAKEAWAYS

1. Make sure that your content includes a story and, if possible, some personal motivations or values. This will help build engagement with the audience.

2. When you come into the room or stand up to deliver your presentation, take a moment to simply connect with the audience. You can also use the floor to ground you at this point; it can help you feel anchored and confident.

3. Try using the connection space tool to give your presentation physical dimension and range.

4. Make sure you orient yourself towards the audience as you deliver your ideas, using eye contact and body language, instead of turning your body towards the slides.

5. If you are preparing a presentation, underline where you wish to make eye contact.

6. An antidote to nerves is good communication – get your objective clear and focus on your audience.

7. Practise, be it through visualization or the real thing will get your brain accustomed to the speech, which in turn will put you at ease and boost your confidence.

8. Remember to choose the fear-busting techniques you like, and rely on them for support during the presentation. Find what works for you.

9. It may be useful to understand your fears, but recognize that they are often unfounded. Use your adult brain to combat those fears, once you understand them.

PART FIVE

FUNDAMENTALS OF BETTER MEETINGS

Meetings are notorious for giving space to the loudest and the brashest, regardless of the quality of their ideas. We all know what it's like when we can't quite do ourselves justice in a meeting. If we are not loud enough, we need to use strategies so that our brilliant ideas reverberate through the static. In this chapter, we explore three areas that are critically important in meetings: how to listen well, how to speak well and how to interrupt and be interrupted – well!

DIFFERENT KINDS OF MEETINGS:

A BATTLEGROUND: This can be a harsh place where people do their best to take others down. If you enter into this kind of skirmish, the only way to come out on top is if you're a louder voice than the others. And even then it's a small victory, as there's no engaged, collegial team to work with at the end.

A MERRY-GO-ROUND: This is the type of meeting that goes on for what seems like an eternity with nothing accomplished at the end of it. People tend to speak, agree, disagree, say why they disagree, come up with the next point, explain why they disagree, come back to the first point, etc. These meetings are as frustrating as they are futile. Again, it's often the loudest voices that spin that wheel.

A FERTILE GROUND: This is the sort of meeting where everyone's voices are encouraged, where collaboration is key and colleagues feel comfortable supporting one another. Although our own ego may be present, the shared vision and goals for the organization are the priority. This is the ideal kind of meeting, where the energy of the gathering itself leads to more creative ideas. In this setting, there is an overall sense that together the team is more powerful than the individual parts and everyone has something valuable to offer. Decisions are made, projects begun, and there is a pervasive feeling of wellbeing and achievement. So this meeting sweet spot is where we want to get to.

Read on to find out how you can do your bit to encourage this.

CHAPTER 1: PREPARE, DELIVER AND SHINE

PREPARING YOUR POINT

Preparation is crucial. To avoid waffling during the meeting, make a list of what you would like to add to the formal schedule in advance. It's worthwhile to get crystal clear on your desired outcome prior to the meeting. This effort will be well rewarded as you come across prepared and polished, and are more likely to achieve your meeting goals. Try plotting out this sort of concise, results-oriented game plan:

1. Hook people's attention by defining the problem that you want to tackle.
2. Explain in clear, focused points how a given idea solves that problem.
3. Describe the actions that need to be taken.
4. Finish up with your proposed action plan which includes the dates of completion.

Prepare for any challenges that might come up. Write these out along with your possible responses. When you've finished speaking, ask for input or questions – this will help propel the meeting forward, prompting buy-in, brainstorming and the formulation of realistic action plans.

VOCAL DELIVERY

Many people feel fine speaking in meetings if they're sufficiently prepared. It is the moments when they need to speak off-the-cuff that they find challenging. If this is you, then here are some simple guidelines to help you.

STEP ONE: Jot down a few points before you speak so you have some sense of what you need to cover. You can use single words or short phrases to jog your memory, and then number them in the order that you want to deliver them. This can take less than a minute to do, yet it will give you invaluable support if your mind goes blank while speaking.

STEP TWO: When you are speaking, remember to use pauses and to deliver your ideas with ample eye contact. By talking steadily (not rushing to get your idea out and your moment over with), you will be able to think as you go, and you will find that your thoughts line up in a far more ordered fashion.

STEP THREE: Don't allow yourself to get rushed by other people. Find a steady pace and speak clearly. Don't get bullied into inadequate phrasing.

TO ASSESS YOUR PERFORMANCE, YOU CAN ASK YOURSELF:

- Do I give myself enough time to find the best words?
- Do I engage with the listeners and paint a picture in their heads?
- Do I seem enthusiastic about what I'm saying?

  If the answer is yes to these, you are off and away.

PHYSICAL DELIVERY

It is worth paying attention to your physical delivery and to have confident body language, since everyone's eyes will be on you as they decide whether you are saying something of value or not.

Sit up straight

This does a few things. It sends signals to your body and brain that you are alert and ready to go, so you will feel more prepared and energized. It gives you access to your diaphragm, which means your voice will come out with increased power. It also helps to show that you respect yourself and are confident.

Smile and make eye contact

The power of a smile is significant, so use it wherever possible. Of course, it must be genuine – if it doesn't feel genuine, avoid it, but try and let your eyes be warm and receptive. Remember that the purpose of a smile is to build connection and warmth with others, which are probably in line with your desired outcomes for the meeting.

Gesture and space

Ensure you are centred in your chair and your shoulders are back. Use your hands to outline and further emphasize your points. Make sure to send the energy outwards rather than inwards. This will help you to own your space, and from there you can let your ideas be heard.

CHAPTER 2: LISTEN UP - IT'S MORE IMPORTANT THAN YOU REALIZE

It is essential to practise active listening in meetings. Listening builds up receptivity, as well as connections with the people in the room. So you should listen as you would like to be listened to: with focused attention, warmth and openness. This means nodding, having an open and non-judgmental face and an awareness that it takes courage to share ideas in public.

LEVELS OF LISTENING IN MEETINGS

There are three levels of listening in meetings and it's good to practise balancing out all three.

LEVEL ONE involves self-oriented listening – waiting for the best opportunity to share your thoughts or ideas. You will need to do some of this, but you certainly don't want to hang out here all the time.

LEVEL TWO entails actively engaging with other people's ideas and understanding their point of view.

LEVEL THREE calls for sitting back and listening for the subtleties underlying other people's words. You will pick up all sorts of interesting dynamics. You might notice the person who is dying to speak but can't find a way to be heard. You may notice the person who's itching to take over the room with their energy. And you might notice the person who is calm and calculating, biding their time. Perhaps that's you?

Being aware of such dynamics will help you to support others, directing your attention not necessarily to the loudest person, but to the one who appears to have something valuable to contribute.

BEING GENEROUS IN MEETINGS

It's important to appreciate that everyone around the table has their own agenda and is operating on a personal set of motivations, values and standards. This will help you to be receptive even when you disagree with what they are saying. It is this awareness that can make the difference between a battleground type meeting or a fertile ground type. So try not to be judgmental when you hear something you disagree with. The other people in the room will be more receptive to you if you handle their ideas (and their egos) gently.

CHAPTER 3: INTERRUPTIONS - CLAIMING YOUR SPACE

Ever been interrupted in a meeting? Probably. Have you ever been interrupted in the middle of a particularly important point, by someone who didn't even seem to notice you were speaking? Likely. Interrupting happens all the time. So how do we handle it while maintaining positive connections?

First, try not to respond to any angry reflexes that make you want to slam your fist on the table and tell them how rude they are. Second, if any negative voices creep into your head – either about yourself, like 'I'm boring,' or about them, like 'they're intolerable' – do your best to bat them away. They are not helpful here. Third, decide if you want to let it go and pick up your point later, or if you want to do something about it here and now. If it's the latter, follow these steps to take back your space:

STEP ONE: You can stop them in their tracks by saying as loudly as necessary something like, 'Excuse me.' This is best said with a low and firm tone, but one that is clearly audible.

STEP TWO: Now you have their attention, hold it for a moment in silence. This is crucial. This is when you take back ownership of the space, claiming your right to speak. In this moment of stillness, you bring the energy and attention back to you. It is also, very importantly, a chance to calm down.

STEP THREE: Now start speaking, using one of the comments below or a few words of your own. The main thing is to ensure you don't speak with anger – just clearly, politely and firmly.

''I'd really like to finish my point, if that's okay with you.'

'I'm sorry, I hadn't quite finished.'

'You interrupted me just now. Would you mind if I finish?'

It's likely that they will apologize and politely (even somewhat awkwardly) concede. If they grumble or appear displeased, be gracious so they know you are not angry, just claiming your space back.

STEP FOUR: Once you have finished your point, thank them for giving you space. That way you are positively reinforcing their good behaviour, and making future interruptions less likely. Avoid making them feel chagrined or smaller for interrupting you. Punishing or embarrassing them is far less productive in terms of leading to desired outcomes.

CHAPTER 4: INTERRUPTING - HANDLE WITH CARE

So the meeting is going at full steam, and there's lots of energy coursing through the room, which is great. But now it's come to the point where you want to say something, and the voices around you are so loud that you're not sure how to do it. Well, there is a simple device you can use to break in.

Interrupt with something nice.

Even the loudest person in the room will be quiet when it comes to listening to something nice directed at them. Start a sentence with 'great', 'yes' or 'that's a fantastic idea' and you create instant receptivity and a warm feeling. If, on the other hand, you start a sentence with a negative, chances are they won't be so inclined to stop speaking. How many times have you heard someone interrupt with 'the problem with that is' or 'no' or 'but'? Would you want to stop talking if you heard any of these?

This isn't just a trick. It is about respecting the process of communication, which is an exchange of ideas, thoughts and feelings between two or more people. It's polite and respectful to receive a person's idea before offering your own. The idea of an interjection that simply interrupts with your own idea is ultimately a selfish one. Yes, you may have something you want to say, but you also need to give them something they want to hear.

TIP: Don't follow the positive statement with a 'but' as that instantly replaces the positive with a negative. It's important to find the positive in what has just been said in order to make people receptive to your idea.

CHAPTER 5: CLEVER TOOLS FOR CLEVERER MEETINGS

The tools listed below can help you to achieve a fertile ground meeting:

1. CHECK-IN AND CHECK-OUT

To help with productivity, and to ensure a climate of listening, try using a quick check-in or check-out process.

At the beginning of the meeting a check-in can be performed by the chairperson, by asking everyone for their key goals and for anything else that they might like to share or discuss. This ensures that everyone gets heard and all ideas are brought to the group's attention.

A check-out can be a few questions that each person is asked. This can be a really solid and collaborative way to close a meeting. For example:

- What is one achievement from this meeting that you are satisfied with?
- What is one acknowledgement you would like to give someone here?

This second point is an incredibly powerful tool that helps create an environment in which people feel recognized, appreciated and supported - it creates a space where they can flourish.

2. LION

Lion stands for Last week's actions, Issues, Opportunities and Next week's actions. It is a useful device for structuring a team meeting.

Last week's actions:	What did you agree to do last week and have you done it yet?
Issues:	Any problem areas identified this week?
Opportunities:	Use KPI's (key performance indicators - measures of incremental success) to show current opportunities that can be taken advantage of.
Next week's actions:	A list of tasks to be undertaken prior to the next team meeting.

3. SMART GOALS IN MEETINGS

Create clear parameters by turning the meeting's desired outcomes into specific, measurable, time-sensitive actions, with clarity on what constitutes positive results. This is called SMART goal-setting, which stands for:

Specific - A clear goal will help you to focus efforts and feel motivated to achieve it.

Measurable - A goal can be tracked for progress, helping you to stay motivated.

Attainable - Your goal also needs to be realistic and achievable. It should stretch your abilities while remaining within the realm of possibility.

Relevant - Ensure that your goal matters to you, and is aligned with other relevant objectives.

Timely - Every goal needs a target date, so that you have a deadline to focus on and something to work towards.

These should be noted and agreed with those involved; you can then follow up on them by email or face-to-face in the next meeting.

You can visit this web link for a deeper dive on the SMART goal-setting methodology:
https://www.mindtools.com/pages/article/smart-goals.htm

PART FIVE TAKEAWAYS

1. Know your core goals for the meeting and stand by thcm.

2. Plan for difficult questions

3. Make sure your body language helps you out - good posture and use of hands send confident signals to your brain and to others.

4. Go in with actions you intend to carry out and any you want for others to carry out clear in your head. Make sure you establish/agree set dates for when you want these achieved.

5. Listen to your colleagues, giving them support, and, in turn, they will be more inclined to listen to you.

6. Always interject with something nice to create receptivity and show respect.

7. If someone interrupts you, stop them, take a moment to neutralize the negative energy and then carry on calmly and without tension.

8. Try the Check-In, Check-Out and the LION techniques for more productive meetings.

9. Prepare what you want to say before the meeting, using SMART goals if you feel they'll be helpful, and have a firm grasp of the outcome you'd like to achieve.

PART **SIX**

FUNDAMENTALS OF BETTER ARGUMENTS

We have all experienced those occasions when a conversation spirals out of control, despite our best intentions. Likewise, we have all been on the receiving end of another person's wrath and, whether we believe it is justified or not, it is never pleasant. Often we go into an argument feeling so assured of our position that we can't imagine anything but the perfect outcome. We're certain the other person will realize how wrong they are, that they'll beg for forgiveness, and that we'll graciously accept their apology. The reality is usually quite different and can lead to a stand-off, with both parties refusing to back down.

In Part Six of this book we offer some helpful tools and techniques, and a new way of thinking about conflict. We propose a departure from the usual right/wrong paradigm and, in its place, offer insights from a powerful methodology called Non-Violent Communication. We'll also provide gems from psychology and the latest in neuroscience.

This section is more practical than philosophical, giving you helpful tools that you can use straight away to diffuse, redirect and transform your most difficult conversations. I have used them constantly through the years, and have helped friends and clients to use them ... and they work!

CHAPTER 1: SEVEN GEMS FOR KEEPING THE PEACE

GEM ONE: DON'T WRITE SOMEONE'S SCRIPT FOR THEM

Have you ever thought someone was annoyed with you, and you in turn have become annoyed with them, without even knowing whether your frustration was justified? Probably. This is typical of 'writing someone's script'. And we all do it! Even though we feel we know what someone is thinking, it's unwise to assume that we can read their thoughts. Sometimes our intuition is borne out, but often times it is not.

Israeli-American psychologist Daniel Kahneman's Nobel Prize-winning book, *Thinking Fast and Slow* (2011, Farrar, Straus and Giroux Publishing), explored this idea. Citing various research, he concluded that contrary to what we think and feel, our instincts are often wrong. So, regardless of how certain you are that you know what someone is thinking, don't let that influence your actions. Instead, get into the habit of asking them what's on their mind. You may be surprised. This alone will help you avoid all manner of difficult situations with people.

GEM TWO: WHAT WE THINK ABOUT, WE MAKE MANIFEST

If you think long and hard enough about something, it will to some degree manifest itself in your real-world experience. If you find yourself thinking you always get into arguments, or are surrounded by argumentative people, then chances are your behaviour will encourage and reinforce that conviction.

The good news is that you can change this. First you must notice that you have these thoughts and then accept that it is within your power to think differently.

If, for example, you enter into a difficult conversation believing that you must prepare for a fight, try simply reframing the situation. Try thinking of it in this way: 'I used to have arguments with people but am now going to engage in – and encourage in others – a more peaceful way of communicating.' Once you have allowed yourself to become aware of the habitual thought, you become open to the possibility of accepting new, entirely different thoughts. And, in doing so, you can break the pattern.

GEM THREE: NEUROPLASTICITY AND TRAINING YOUR BRAIN

We have the power to change the way we think. In the last ten years, huge discoveries have been made around the neuroplasticity of the brain. Scientists have found that there is always potential for brain development. This can be as simple as learning new skills, or as complex as training a part of your brain to literally change its functionality. This means that while our beliefs and patterns of behaviour become hard-wired into our brains, you can at any point re-wire a new set of beliefs and behavioural patterns.

If you find that you are always getting into arguments, you can use the methods described in the next few chapters to break the cycle. By practising these repeatedly, after some time you will discover that the new patterns have become second nature.

GEM FOUR: THE ANGRY AMYGDALA

As the human brain evolved, one of its earliest parts was the amygdala, which, among other things, houses our fight-or-flight reflex – the basic physiological reaction to a perceived threat. As our brains continued to develop, the cerebral cortex took shape, giving us our ability to make rational judgments by logically thinking things through.

If something happens that makes us angry, it is our amygdala that kicks in first. If we act from here, actions tend to be impulsive and can easily lead to a dangerous spiral of anger. If we can wait a few seconds, our higher-functioning cerebral cortex kicks in, allowing us to make more well-reasoned judgments about the best approach. So if something riles you, don't let yourself be guided by your angry amygdala. Instead, take a breath, count to five and allow your cerebral cortex to move back into the driving seat.

GEM FIVE: PEOPLE WANT TO FEEL RECOGNIZED

If you want to resolve something peacefully, begin by making sure that you hear, understand and acknowledge the people you're dealing with. Even if you don't agree with them, this will create fertile ground for negotiation and consensus. By doing this you will take them out of a defensive or offensive space and into a space of openness. People are not going to be as quick or eager to disagree with you if you make the effort to understand and recognize their position. If you can start here, in any difficult conversation, then you are starting at a place of peace. This approach is at the core of non-violent communication, which we'll examine more closely in the next few chapters.

GEM SIX: IMPORTANCE OF TONE OF VOICE

When you are speaking, watch your tone. If you refuse to raise your voice to a loud volume, the other person will likely keep their voice down to a reasonable level as well. One of the most challenging things with anger is avoiding getting caught up in its dark energy. Keeping your tone of voice steady is a good way to manage this.

GEM SEVEN: EMPOWER THEM

A fantastic way to motivate and get the best out of someone is to empower them. Replacing anger with an empowering approach not only leads to two people feeling good but is, in the long run, far more productive. Putting responsibility in their hands to rectify the problem, come up with a solution or step up in some way is a great way to change angry energy into empowering energy. So asking them how they can resolve the issue, or giving them additional responsibility, will demonstrate your faith in them and cast the entire conversation in a different light.

CHAPTER 2: THE WORLD OF NON-VIOLENT COMMUNICATION

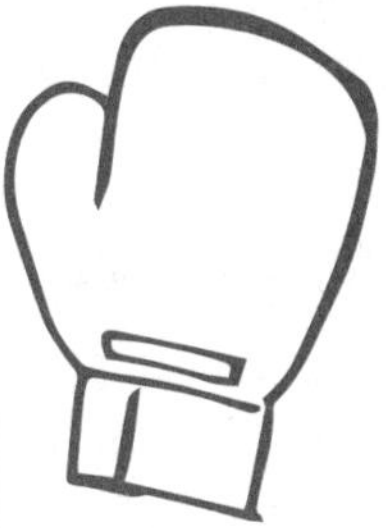

A difficult conversation that goes wrong can lead to a cacophony of negative emotions. There are few inevitable outcomes, and they're all less than desirable:

- Everyone is angry.
- There is a winner and a loser.
- The loser either feels like a victim - mistreated, bitter and resentful - or they're quietly simmering and biding their time.
- The winner may feel powerful, but it's an unhealthy power. It is the power of warfare - tinged with aggression and dominance - and one battle follows another unless a peace accord is struck.

An entirely different approach is geared towards eliminating warfare, attacks and counter-attacks, power struggles, victims and vanquishers. With this way of thinking, successfully dealing with conflict is not about winning, it is about peace, reconciliation and mutual respect.

The Non-Violent Communication (NVC) method was developed by American psychologist Marshall Rosenberg in the 1940s and has been used to resolve all kinds of conflict, from marital discord to strife in the Middle East. Its four tenets, described below, require a paradigm shift that is both radical and yet incredibly wise.

TENET ONE: THERE IS NO RIGHT AND WRONG

If we want to arrive at a peaceful resolution, we have to let go of our notions of right and wrong. In most arguments, we tend to go in with the idea that we are right and the other party is wrong. If we didn't believe this, there would be little point in fighting our corner. While it may be logical, this outlook is not conducive to a peaceful outcome. It's a very human position to take, but it's not in the least bit helpful. Rosenberg held that there is little to be achieved through the right/wrong paradigm and that even if you come out a winner, you leave with a thin triumph of the ego, rather than a healthy communication transaction. In addition, if there is a winner, there is also a loser. Since nobody wants to be wrong, they either submit under a cloud of negative emotions or fight to make themselves right.

Therefore, in order to achieve peace we need to let go of right and wrong.

TENET TWO: ALL ACTIONS ARE STRATEGIES AROUND MET OR UNMET VALUES AND NEEDS

If we let go of right and wrong, what is there? The answer is simple and it starts with understanding.

The NVC approach states that at the core of all actions are fundamental human values and needs, such as love, respect, achievement and connection and all of these values and needs are equal.

It also states that every single action we take is the result of trying to get our values and needs met, or a response to them not being met. When we disagree with someone, this approach asks us to try and understand the values underlying their actions, rather than automatically judge them as wrong.

John Assaraf, an Israeli-Canadian motivational speaker, author and philanthropist, says that most arguments emerge simply from a difference in values. If you can respect that different people have different values, it's a great start to good communication. That doesn't mean the outcome is always going to be easy to reach, but it lays a foundation of respect and empathy.

TENET THREE: THERE ARE NO WRONG ACTIONS, JUST INEFFECTIVE STRATEGIES

Rosenberg also argued that there are no right and wrong actions. Rather, there are effective and ineffective strategies. So if someone does something that seems particularly awful, rather than calling it bad we should consider the underlying value that led to that person's strategy. For example, a gang member is desperate to belong, so he may do terrible things to be part of the crew. His disturbing deeds do not make him wrong – they're strategic gambits to fulfill a need, which in this case is to be loved or feel that he belongs. The strategies may be ineffective, in that he may end up in prison feeling more alone than before. But through the lens of NVC there is no focus on him being wrong.

This idea helps us to gain empathy and to understand other people's actions, even really horrible ones.

TENET FOUR: THE WAY TO PEACE IS TO BE AN ADVOCATE OF OUR OWN VALUES AND THE OTHER PERSON'S VALUES

This final tenet is quite beautiful. It asks us to understand the values motivating the other person's behaviour in a conflict situation, and become an advocate of both their values and our own. This call for mutual respect paves the way for forgiveness and for peaceful resolution.

If you like the sound of this, read on.

CHAPTER 3: IF YOU'RE ANGRY AND YOU KNOW IT ...

What do you do when you have something difficult to say to someone? Blurt it right out? Build yourself into a state of vexation until you are so angry with them you don't care how they react? Give it a half-hearted pass and come out of the conversation furious at yourself for not having said what you needed to say?

Difficult conversations are challenging for everyone. Many people dislike confrontation so much that they will do anything to avoid it, even side-stepping a tough situation entirely instead of confronting it. Here is another way to have a difficult conversation that doesn't result in anger on your part or defensiveness on the other party's.

STEP ONE: ATTITUDE SHIFT

Something has happened and you are angry. You don't like how an employee has behaved, how a friend has treated you, something a colleague has done. You may want to tell them about their mistakes and why you are annoyed. However, as we know, that is going into the zone of right and wrong. All that will do is create the unfertile soil of fear.

The first thing you need to do, before approaching them, is shift your attitude to one that recognizes everyone for doing their best to meet their own needs.

This means feeling your anger, but also being prepared to formulate an understanding of what is going on for the other person.

ASK YOURSELF: Why am I so annoyed here? What values are not getting met? What might be going on for the other person? What values or needs are they honouring by behaving the way they're behaving? What, if any, values and needs might not be getting met?

STEP TWO: RECOGNITION AND ACKNOWLEDGEMENT

So you are now face-to-face with the person who has angered you. Don't leap in with your gripe. Start with a moment of recognition if you can. People thrive on praise and wither in the face of criticism. If you begin a difficult conversation by recognizing what the person is doing well, you create receptivity for whatever you are about to say.

If we see the good in people, they are more likely to behave in that way, whereas if we label someone as a bad person, then it's more likely they will act that way.

So if you need to give someone a formal warning, or tell them their work isn't good enough, or air a grievance on a personal level, start by saying something that shows that you see good in them. This can be a game-changing first step.

ASK YOURSELF: What are their values? Where are they doing really well?

STEP THREE: LISTENING TO THE OTHER PERSON

Knowing what's going on with the other person puts you in a more informed position. So be prepared to ask some open questions and find out their side of the story.

If you think you know which values or needs are driving them, ask them if that is indeed the case. If you don't know what values are driving their actions, then ask questions to find out. It might be that your values are so different that you can't find a middle ground. But at least you can part company with mutual respect. Remember, all values are equal. Once you've heard what is going on with them, you are likely to feel more empathy and understanding, and that will help you to be less judgmental or aggressive.

The other person could get aggressive, depending on if they too have been harbouring ill feelings. If this happens, it's important to manage the situation calmly and prevent it from going badly. Again, it can be as simple as acknowledging that you've heard them and their position.

ASK THEM: What do you think? How do you feel this or that is going?

STEP FOUR: SHARING YOUR POSITION

When you share your position, it's important that you reveal the circumstances that have lead to your feelings. Prior to the discussion, get clear on what the issue is, which values aren't being met (if you haven't done this in step one) and what the other person's actions were that caused the issue for you. List out the facts. There should be no judgment, no evaluation and no subjective terms creeping in. Don't mix the hard, cold facts up with your emotional, subjective evaluation of the facts.

This is crucial because it takes the emotion out of the situation and distils things down to a set of irrefutable facts. It's difficult to do, though, and as soon as you introduce subjective terms, the other person can start to react. So really try and watch yourself here!

ASK YOURSELF: What are the actual facts and events that led to the problem? What is an objective and neutral description of the situation?

STEP FIVE: SHARING YOUR VALUES AND NEEDS OR FEELINGS

State your own values and needs, and point out where they are not being met, but do it without assigning blame. This means you take responsibility for your feelings and your needs, owning them as yours. Use language like 'I feel', rather than 'you did' to avoid judgment and accusation. And by expressing your feelings, there is an element of honesty and responsibility, which takes the heat out of it for the listener and helps them to hear you better.

ASK YOURSELF: What do you feel? Are you frustrated, upset, annoyed, disappointed? Examine why you feel that way. What needs or values have not been met?

STEP SIX: REQUEST WHAT YOU WOULD LIKE MOVING FORWARD

This is the point where you ask for the actions that you believe will make it better. You won't necessarily get them but, by asking, you can really move things forward. This is the most productive and simple step, but also the most difficult because it makes us feel vulnerable.

It takes courage to state what we really want, bestowing upon the other person the power to grant it or not. The risk, of course, is that they may say no. It also means we move to a place that is receptive to finding harmony and compromise, and that can be a tough transition for anyone to make.

ASK YOURSELF: What is it you would like them to do? What are the simple actions they could take that would mean your need or value is met?

CHAPTER 4: BIG BAD WOLF

It's not easy or pleasant being in the firing line, but these steps will help you to resist the slings and arrows of someone else's anger, whether you deserve them or not. They will also help keep you calm, avoid some of the cardinal sins and give you the tools to come out with a more productive relationship ... or, at least, emerge relatively unscathed.

The steps described here are, unsurprisingly, very similar to those employed in handling your own anger. One of the biggest skills here is listening and not immediately reacting, which can take some practice and a lot of long, slow breathing!

STEP ONE: LISTEN

At the moment you are attacked, you might find that you have an initial fight-or-flight reaction. It's important you don't react straight away. If you feel a surge of anger, breathe a little and wait for it to pass. Take a breath deep into your belly and focus on the exhale; count to five in your head as you breathe out. By this time, you are likely to feel like you're back in control.

Once control has been regained, all you need to do is listen. It's important that you don't absorb the other person's energy but, if you can, just sit and hear them out until they've got it off their chest.

Avoid the temptation to defend yourself. Your body doesn't need to be tense – in fact, the more relaxed you are, the less prone you'll be to getting caught up in their angry energy. Again, managing your breathing will help to keep you calm.

Even if you think the person accusing you is totally unjustified, try to understand where they are coming from. If you automatically write them off as wrong or unreasonable, that will usually heighten their anger and fuel their attack. Better to try and get your head around where they are and what has annoyed them. In what way are their values not being met?

TIP: If you feel up to it, you can make a gentle 'ahh' sound, subtly nod, or say anything relatively neutral and meaningless like 'okay' or 'right'. This will help them feel that they've been heard and calm them down more quickly.

STEP TWO: SEEK FURTHER UNDERSTANDING

This is your opportunity to seek additional clarification if you don't fully understand their anger. It helps you to show that you are really engaging with their issue. It also gives them a chance to speak and further diffuse the situation. From your point of view, you cannot move towards an apology or resolve a situation you are not sure about. To find out more, you can use lines like these:

It sounds like x is the problem, is that right?
From what I understand, xx has happened, is that the case?
Are you saying ...? So you feel that ...?
It sounds like you've been pretty frustrated, man.
Will you tell me more about what's going on.

Now, wait while they respond. They may be rude and aggressive again, or they may have calmed down. If you feel they are being too abusive, simply and calmly make clear that while you are happy to listen, you are not willing to be spoken to in a rude manner. This is about listening and mutual respect; it's not about being a doormat.

TIP: The key here is a calm tone. So make sure you speak slowly and in a low voice, so as to not enter the 'battleground'.

STEP THREE: EMPATHY AND/OR RECOGNITION

Whatever the relationship – whether you're engaged with an employee, a client or your superior – the basics always apply. Your first sentence after they have finished speaking should include two things: acknowledgement that you have heard them, and empathy for their situation. They can't then tell you that you don't understand where they're coming from.

This will literally take the wind out of their sails. If you give them nothing for their anger to stick to, eventually they will cool off enough to have a normal conversation.

STEP FOUR: SHARING AND TAKING RESPONSIBILITY

Finally, state your position. Whether you did something or didn't, or have a different perspective on things, or zealously disagree, the most important thing is to not step into right and wrong territory. There are three options here:

You take responsibility

You offer a solution and tell them what you intend to do and in what time frame, then follow up with a question to check in. This is a very powerful way of calming someone down.

They have the wrong end of the stick

You now need to explain your position. Keep your voice calm and steady. If the other party's being terse or loud, don't get sucked into matching their tone and volume unless you do it strategically. It is important to choose wording that shows that you understand their position, whether you agree with it or not. Remember, explanation can only come after acknowledgement.

It is your responsibility

If you think you are to blame, take it on the chin. Even if there are extenuating circumstances (and there usually are), take responsibility. You can do it while still being totally respectful of your own values. Taking responsibility means respecting their values and owning your actions. See the next section for how to manage apologies.

CHAPTER 5: SORRY - SOME WORDS DON'T COME EASILY ...

The apology is a territory that needs to be negotiated carefully, to maintain personal integrity while being respectful of others. But it's possible to do both! Remember, be an advocate of your own values and the other person's values. (On a personal note, I believe the key to a caring and contented life lies in this powerful statement.)

Be sparing with your apologies, not least because there are only two reasons to apologize: either for your actions or for the impact they have on someone's feelings. There is a lot of power at play in those words and they need to be handled carefully. Try not to over-use the word 'sorry' as it can lead to either feeling like a doormat or coming across as insincere.

Having said that, if you have done something wrong, a simple apology can be the easiest way to diffuse the situation. 'I'm so sorry I was late' can make all the difference. You don't need to lose your power in an apology.

APOLOGIZING FOR YOUR ACTIONS

Only do this if you have something to take responsibility for. If this is the case, make sure your 'sorry' is clear and specific rather than a vague nod to being wrong. Don't let it be just a word. Rather than just, 'I'm sorry,' explain what you are apologizing for. For instance, 'I realize that I should have told you sooner. That was a mistake and I'm sorry.'

APOLOGIZING FOR THEIR FEELINGS

This is a compromise apology, best deployed when you don't feel you need to apologize for your actions, but the other person is clearly upset or angry. This way you can maintain your integrity but give them a placating word they may desperately need. Still, it must be genuine or you'll simply make matters worse. With this apology you are delivering empathy for their feelings and understanding for their values and view points. ('I can see that you're hurt and I'm so sorry about that. I apologize.')

TIP: If you find apologizing difficult, try to understand the other party's pain and why they are upset. Then your apology can be genuine and not a fall-back reaction to being backed into a corner.

PART SIX TAKEAWAYS

1. Breathing helps you move to the cerebral cortex and deal with angry impulses.

2. Don't go in with expectations about what is going on with the other person. Be prepared to find out.

3. Think about why you're annoyed. Which values and needs are not being met?

4. Think about why they might be behaving in the way they are. What values or needs might they be honouring by their behaviour?

5. Be prepared to find something positive in their behaviour, so they know you are not wantonly criticizing them for the sake of it.

6. Be clear on your request to them, and use an empowering question (if appropriate) to involve them in the solution.

7. Whether you agree or disagree with the person who's on the attack, make sure to use empathy and acknowledgement before you state your position.

8. Be careful with the word 'sorry'. It's important that you say it with integrity.

9. Remember to be an advocate of your own *and* the other person's values. That is the way to a peaceful resolution.

CONCLUSION

Here's a master list of what you should avoid in your interpersonal communication:

WHAT TO AVOID IN YOUR SPEECH

AVOID 'YOU' PHRASES IN CONFRONTATION SITUATIONS: These can antagonize your sparring partner, and push them straight into the defensive. Instead of telling them what they did, refer to how it makes you feel.

AVOID TOO MANY 'I'S IN EMAILS - IT MAKES YOU SOUND SELF-CENTRED: A well-established theatre director I once wrote to back in my theatre days finally responded to my hounding emails and met me for lunch. After an hour of excellent conversation, he dropped the bombshell. 'You repeated 'I' 37 times in your email,' he said. (Ever since then, I've assiduously avoided the mistake of the most famous pronoun.)

AVOID TALKING IN INTERVIEWS WITHOUT KNOWING WHERE YOU ARE GOING: You never want the interviewer to wish the ground would swallow them up while you rattle on, trapped in a story that you no longer know why you are telling but feel you can't get out of.

AVOID BEING A GENERALIST AND TOO SAFE: Instead, bring yourself and your personal experiences, anecdotes, values and feelings into your communication. There is room for that special bit of you everywhere, from the one-to-one meeting to the public speech and everything in between.

WHAT TO AVOID IN YOUR BODY

AVOID CROSSED ARMS: This is not a powerful position, just a closed one. It makes people feel as though you are shut off and removed from the situation. Instead, hold your hands at your navel or hang them at your sides. Or, if they really feel like a couple of dangly things attached to your shoulders, you can place one hand in your pocket, or hold a notebook.

AVOID SLUMPED SHOULDERS: Especially when entering a room or starting a speech or presentation, this posture gives a negative impression – and that first impression is crucial! Instead, roll your shoulders back or stroke them open with your fingers. That tiny difference makes a disproportionate improvement and is well worth it.

AVOID LIMP HANDSHAKES: Who wants to hold a dead fish? Instead, go firm. Put your enthusiasm for opening this new channel of communication into your hand and shake with confidence and conviction. You will have an intention as you engage in every conversation – it might be landing a job, impressing the person or just the satisfaction of connecting with someone new. Whatever your objective, let your pursuit of it be purposeful, and let that be reflected in your handshake.

AVOID BREAKING EYE CONTACT: Eye contact can feel scary and revealing, yet avoiding it is even more revealing. If you can't look someone in the eye, you are effectively giving them licence to think all sorts of things about you that you have no control over.

AVOID CLENCHING YOUR JAW, GRITTING YOUR TEETH OR FROWNING: Unless you want the other person to mirror your body language – in which case they will get defensive or shut themselves down entirely – always avoid these negative signals. It's a bit like a poker player's 'tell'. You need to know what signals you are giving so you can be in control of them. Instead, do a big yawn, relax your mouth, smile to get those muscles working and imagine the warm sun shining on your face. Adopt an attitude of receptivity and openness, and let your face reflect it. In most cases you'll benefit from this. At the very least, your cards will be held more tightly to your chest.

AVOID FIDDLING IN MEETINGS OR INTERVIEWS; AGAIN, IT'S LIKE DISPLAYING YOUR EMOTIONS ON A PROJECTION SCREEN: Instead, make sure you are grounded and centred on the chair, using the floor to support you and give you energy. Use your hands to gesticulate to the extent that it feels natural.

WHAT TO AVOID IN YOUR VOICE

AVOID SPEAKING AT THE PACE OF YOUR THOUGHTS, WHICH IS BOUND TO BE TOO FAST: You only get to do this when you are enunciating with utmost clarity and when you have your audience or listeners firmly with you, running alongside you in the frenzied adrenaline rush of the moment. For a perfect visual of this, watch Charlie Chaplin's speech in *The Great Dictator*, where he begins slowly and then spends 45 seconds in a high-energy climax; it is spellbinding. https://www.youtube.com/watch?v=w8HdOHrc3OQ

AVOID A MONOTONE: Don't drag your voice along as if you have no energy to pull it off the floor. Again, if you do that, people will feel like you don't care about what you are saying.

AVOID LONG, COMPLICATED SENTENCES: Don't put too many clauses in a thought, and be careful not to swing upward at the end of the points you're making. Instead, use vocal gravity and unit breaks to deliver each mini-idea.

AVOID MAKING ALL WORDS EQUAL: Try not to pronounce grammatical connector words with the same emphasis that you use for important words. Instead, find the key words that hold your meaning and put your energy into those!

AVOID MUMBLING OR UNDER-ARTICULATING: Your listener will want to hear what you say without straining. Instead, do your vocal warm-ups and practice speaking clearly with your knuckle in between your teeth!

AVOID SPEAKING WITH YOUR MOUTH BARELY OPEN: Incarcerating the soul of your words inside your mouth will achieve nothing. Instead, open your mouth and release the emotion around the vowels of those words that are important to you.

AUTHOR'S NOTE:

The idea of *The Connection Book* is to give you tips and insights, in whatever area of communication you need. Whether it's getting through a sticky spot, or finding a new perspective, or opening up a relationship or situation that seems blocked.

In other words, it is my wish that this book is like a little friend, to support you to make the changes to your communication and connections that will enhance your life and help you achieve your goals. I sincerely hope I have achieved this goal, and that you have found practical use for the tips and insights within. For the contents of this book are not theoretical, they are about as practical as it gets; we get to practise connecting and communicating every day. The really great thing is that every moment we can choose to change the status quo, we can improve ourselves, we can shift and break habits that aren't working for us. A mountain is climbed in a thousand steps and a totally new direction can start with a half inch pivot.

So whether the changes you would like to make are big or small, starting with one simple change that takes your fancy is a brilliant step.

ABOUT THE AUTHOR

EMMA SERLIN is the director and founder of London Speech Workshop. Prior to setting up London Speech Workshop in 2009 she worked in TV drama as a script and story editor, completed a psychology masters, trained as an actor and was also an award winning theatre director and producer. She is also a certified life coach.

She has infused her various influences into the unique approach to communication that London Speech Workshop delivers to one to one and corporate clients. Their courses increases personal effectiveness through effective communication, presentation skills and accent softening training.